THE MODERN TEEN'S HANDBOOK: CULTIVATING CLARITY AND CRITICAL THINKING IN THE DIGITAL AGE

A Guide to Supporting and Empowering
Young Minds Through
Online Challenges and Opportunities

Featuring:
35+ Case Studies, 20+ Practical Exercises,
Effective Strategies, Essential Tips and Tools

LLR ACADEMY

Copyright © 2024 by LLR Academy

All rights reserved.

No portion of this book may be reproduced in any form without written permission from the publisher or author, except as permitted by U.S. copyright law.

This publication is designed to provide accurate and authoritative information in regard to the subject matter covered. It is sold with the understanding that neither the author nor the publisher is engaged in rendering legal, investment, accounting or other professional services. While the publisher and author have used their best efforts in preparing this book, they make no representations or warranties with respect to the accuracy or completeness of the contents of this book and specifically disclaim any implied warranties of merchantability or fitness for a particular purpose. No warranty may be created or extended by sales representatives or written sales materials. The advice and strategies contained herein may not be suitable for your situation. You should consult with a professional when appropriate. Neither the publisher nor the author shall be liable for any loss of profit or any other commercial damages, including but not limited to special, incidental, consequential, personal, or other damages.

ISBN 978-1-0688573-0-0 (paperback)
ISBN 978-1-0688573-3-1 (hardcover)
ISBN 978-1-0688573-1-7 (ebook)

First Edition

PRAISE FOR
THE MODERN TEEN'S HANDBOOK: CULTIVATING CLARITY AND CRITICAL THINKING IN THE DIGITAL AGE

"In the Internet era, teenagers navigate a vast digital space where they encounter a deluge of valuable and non-useful information. *'The Modern Teen's Handbook'* aims to illuminate how to identify misinformation in the digital landscape. It also addresses several challenges. The book also emphasizes the importance of keeping up with and tracking technological advancements while knowing their drawbacks and benefits. Most importantly the book did not rely solely on theoretical info but also incorporated numerous practical exercises to master digital literacy. I agree that it is worth reading and exercising." — **Dr. Ehab ATTA, Assistant Professor, Curriculum & Material Development, Fatif Sultan Mehmet Vakif University, Turkey**

"The Modern Teen's Handbook: Cultivating Clarity and Critical Thinking in the Digital Age is absolutely essential reading for teens, parents, educators who are looking to properly navigate the complicated digital world we have created. There is no topic that is not covered with style and clarity! You simply will not find a better, more comprehensive resource. I would even say it is for anyone who wants to make a digital change in the digital age." — **Michelle Côté, Highschool Teacher, DCDSB, Pickering**

"As an educator & concerned individual, I wholeheartedly recommend 'The Modern Teen's Handbook' which provides essential guidance for parents, educators, and anyone navigating the digital landscape with teens. In today's rapidly evolving digital world, critical thinking skills are more crucial than ever. In a world where digital literacy is paramount, this handbook bridges the gap between theory and practice. It's a beacon guiding us through the digital maze, ensuring our teens emerge as informed, discerning, and empowered digital citizens. So, dive in, explore, & empower the nextgen—it's a journey worth taking!" — **Dr. Nader Sadek, Ph.D., MBA, BDS, CTDP, McInst.M, Professor/ Consultant, Learning & Development, and HRM Strategist, Toronto**

"As a leadership trainer and certified coach, I am thoroughly impressed with this book. The skills, strategies, and tools presented are so necessary right now, as they take a proactive approach to a virtually connected world that is in dire need of pause and reflection. Equip yourself, your children, and even your team members to navigate our digital world through the inherent wisdom in these pages." — **Julie Dupont, M.A., MCOD, ACC, Principal Strategist, Reimagine Leadership, Cambridge**

"The Modern Teen's Handbook is a must-read for today's teens! It's packed with practical tips, real-life stories, and helpful advice to boost confidence and tackle everyday challenges. Super engaging and incredibly useful – I highly recommend it!" — **Winston Tang, HR Generalist, Toronto**

"Amidst the barrage of information overload and instant communication, it is refreshing to read 'The Modern Teen's Handbook' that lays down basic rules for digital engagement to simplify our lives in this digital world. Also reflects the author's genuine, noble and valiant attempt to help develop a civil and empathetic digital community, to help youngsters avoid the negative impact of digital life on their physical and mental health and to guide them to recognize opportunities of intellectual growth for a brighter future. Whether you are a boomer, blown into the storm of digital world, Gen X that has grown into it or Gen Z that was born into it, this book will be of great help for you to navigate in the "Wild West" of internet and incessant inescapable and at times intimidating instant communications." — **Dr. Shah Nawaz MD, FRCP(C) (Retd), Toronto**

"'The Modern Teen's Handbook' is a guide to thriving and navigating the complexities of today's digital world. From managing information overload to enhancing emotional intelligence online, this book provides a comprehensive toolkit for success. With real-life case studies and actionable advice, readers will learn how to prioritize tasks, manage finances, prioritize well-being, and cultivate critical thinking skills. Whether you're looking to boost productivity, improve digital interactions, or prepare for adulthood in the digital era, this is your ultimate guide to thriving in the fast-paced digital landscape." — **Angela Tucker, Master of Arts in Teaching, Mom of two and a School Teacher to many, Texas**

Glad you're here!

Welcome to an empowering journey with the LLR Academy through the insights and guidance offered in this book. As you embark on this path, remember that every page you turn equips you with the essential skills in clarity and critical thinking to navigate the complexities of the digital world.

This handbook offers **35+** case studies, **20+** practical exercises, effective strategies, essential tips and tools, serving as a beacon for teens in the modern era. We envision a generation capable of discerning truth from misinformation, making informed decisions, and fostering meaningful connections online.

Through this book, we aim to cultivate a community of thoughtful, resilient, and empathetic individuals, prepared to thrive in the digital age's challenges.

We have also added a **Reader's Review Page** at the end of the book, your experience and opinions not only matter to us, but they can also help shape future editions and new titles.

Thank you for choosing to grow with us.

Let's **Learn, Lead,** and **Rise** together.

Contents

INTRODUCTION	1
1. Navigating the Information Overload	7
2. Enhancing Emotional Intelligence in the Digital Realm	27
3. Mastering Time Management and Productivity	43
4. Financial Literacy for the Modern Teen	57
5. Physical and Mental Well-being in a Digital Age	77
6. The Ethics of Digital Life	95
7. Critical Thinking Skills for the Digital World	111
8. Preparing for Digital Adulthood	123
CONCLUSION	135
BONUS EXCERCISES	139
REFRECNCES	150
BONUS QUOTES	151

INTRODUCTION
Book at a Glance

Welcome to *The Modern Teen's Handbook: Cultivating Clarity and Critical Thinking in the Digital Age.* If you're a teen today, you're growing up in a world where digital technology is a constant presence—always on, always connected. This presents incredible opportunities but also real challenges.

On the one hand, you have access to more information and ways to connect with others than any previous generation. You can learn about any topic that interests you, express your creativity in ways that reach a global audience, and build communities with people who share your passions—all with a few taps on a screen. It's an exciting time to be alive.

However, this non-stop stream of content can also be overwhelming. With so many voices clamoring for your attention, it's hard to cut through the noise and find what's true, reliable, and meaningful. You might feel pressure to keep up with the latest trends or present a perfect image online. The constant barrage of information and social comparison can take a toll on your mental health and sense of self. Not to mention, the digital landscape is always changing, so just when you feel like you've got a handle on things, the ground shifts beneath your feet.

To thrive in this environment—to make the most of the opportunities and navigate the challenges—being able to think clearly and critically is a must-have skill. It's the foundation for everything else. But here's the thing: It's not a skill that's often explicitly taught, especially in the context of digital life. That's where this book comes in. Consider it your user manual for developing a strong, agile, and discerning mind in the digital age. Engage with it actively and openly. Question it. Make it your own. And know that with every chapter you read, every strategy you try, every reflective conversation you have, you're not simply learning skills; you're growing in self-awareness, perspective, and agency. You're becoming more of who you want to be—online and off.

Highlights from each chapter:

Chapter 1: "Navigating the Information Overload" equips teens with strategies to handle the constant flood of digital information.

- It covers understanding algorithms and their role in creating echo chambers, with a case study on Lila from Chicago, who broadens her views on environmental issues by exploring diverse perspectives.

- The chapter emphasizes the importance of intentional attention and suggests exercises like the Attention Audit to evaluate the impact of digital consumption.

- It also provides tips on identifying misinformation and managing digital clutter, exemplified by Marcus's journey toward improved mental health and productivity.

This chapter aims to transform information overload into an opportunity for deliberate and informed engagement.

Chapter 2: "Enhancing Emotional Intelligence in the Digital Realm" delves into developing essential emotional skills for online interactions.

- It defines digital emotional intelligence as the ability to communicate authentically and empathetically online while setting healthy boundaries.

- The chapter highlights the use of emojis as tools for expressing emotions and enhancing digital communication.

- It also explores developing digital empathy through understanding emotions behind the screen and provides strategies for handling online conflicts with mindfulness and empathy.

- This chapter offers practical advice on improving digital interactions and managing emotional challenges in the digital world.

Chapter 3: "Mastering Time Management and Productivity" tackles the teenage challenge of balancing academics, social media, and sleep.

- It stresses the importance of prioritizing tasks, suggesting structured scheduling and tools like the Pomodoro Technique, Trello, and Forest to boost focus and productivity.

- The chapter advises against multitasking and promotes "unitasking" as a more effective way to maintain productivity and reduce stress.

- It guides readers in implementing these strategies through real-life examples and practical exercises, such as the Single-Tab Challenge and Time-Block Planner.

The chapter encourages a balanced lifestyle, emphasizing the inclusion of rest and personal interests to enhance overall well-being.

Chapter 4: "Financial Literacy for the Modern Teen" explores managing finances effectively in a digital world.

- It highlights the importance of understanding digital transactions and introduces essential budgeting skills, such as tracking income and expenses and setting realistic financial goals.

- The chapter underscores the value of financial literacy through a case study of Jordan, a teen who learns financial discipline through budgeting.

- It also provides insights into cryptocurrency, advising caution due to its risks, and educates on avoiding online scams like phishing.

The chapter concludes with a critical view on financial influencers, urging teens to scrutinize the credibility of online financial advice. This equips readers with the knowledge to make informed financial decisions and develop sound financial habits.

Chapter 5: "Physical and Mental Well-being in a Digital Age" addresses the benefits and challenges of technology in maintaining health.

- It covers strategies for managing screen time, utilizing technology to support physical fitness, and coping with digital stress and the effects of social media on self-esteem.

- Key tips include performing digital detoxes, establishing digital curfews, and maintaining screen-free zones to improve sleep.

- Case studies illustrate practical applications like Kira's experience improving her sleep and well-being.

The chapter also explores using technology for fitness through apps and online communities and supports mental health with tools like meditation and nutrition tracking apps. This comprehensive guide helps navigate health in a digital world mindfully and strategically.

Chapter 6: "The Ethics of Digital Life" examines the impact of our online behaviors and underscores the need for ethical conduct in digital interactions.

- It focuses on managing digital footprints with attention to privacy and security, combating cyberbullying, responsible content sharing, understanding online consent, and using digital platforms for positive activism.

- The chapter offers practical tips for maintaining privacy, such as using strong passwords and being alert to phishing attempts.

- It also addresses the consequences of cyberbullying and the importance of sharing content responsibly to prevent misinformation.

- It illustrates the repercussions of unethical behavior and the benefits of principled digital conduct through real-world examples.

The chapter advocates for a compassionate online culture, encouraging readers to use their digital presence to promote positive change and treat others with respect and kindness.

Chapter 7: "Critical Thinking Skills for the Digital World" underscores the necessity of critical thinking in evaluating the vast array of online information.

- It emphasizes questioning sources and using logical reasoning to dissect arguments on social media and encourages looking beyond superficial search results to find in-depth information.

- Highlighting the importance of recognizing biases, a case study shows a teen learning about political perspectives by engaging with diverse media.

- Another example illustrates the need for skepticism toward online influencers, prompting verification of their authenticity.

The chapter concludes with resources to enhance critical thinking, such as fact-checking websites and media literacy organizations, equipping teens to navigate digital spaces more thoughtfully and effectively.

Chapter 8: "Preparing for Digital Adulthood" guides teenagers in cultivating their online presence and digital skills for adulthood, focusing on strategically managing their digital identity for future educational and career goals.

- It highlights the importance of a well-curated online presence through case studies like London's effective LinkedIn use and Dax's successful podcast.

The chapter underscores acquiring diverse digital skills, digital security, continuous learning, and balanced tech usage, illustrated by teens like Emma, Austin, Sophia, and Evan.

Overall, it provides a framework for teens to manage their digital lives responsibly, preparing them for future challenges and opportunities. This book is packed with tools, tips, and exercises to help you thrive in today's fast-paced digital environment. From mastering your online presence to developing skills for the future of work.

Chapter 1

Navigating the Information Overload

"Surf the waves of information but anchor your mind in what truly matters. Not all that buzzes is gold." -- LLR Academy

Welcome to the digital age, where information is everywhere, and it's coming at you fast. As a teen in today's world, you're bombarded with a constant stream of news, opinions, memes, and cat videos—it's a lot to take in. But don't worry; this chapter is here to help you make sense of it all and become a master at navigating the digital flood.

Picture this: You're scrolling through your social media feed, and it's like a never-ending waterfall of posts. It's easy to get swept away in the current and lose track of what's important. That's where information filtration comes in—it's the art of sifting through the noise to find the gold.

First off, let's talk algorithms. You know how your feed seems to magically show you stuff you're interested in? That's because platforms like Instagram and TikTok use algorithms to learn what you like and serve you more of it. But here's the thing: These algorithms can also create echo chambers, where you only see content that confirms your existing beliefs. To break out of this bubble, try following accounts with diverse perspectives and engaging with content that challenges your assumptions.

 ### Case Study 1: Echo Chambers and Expanding Your Horizons

Lila, a 16-year-old from Toronto, was passionate about environmental activism. She followed dozens of eco-friendly accounts on social media and loved engaging with content about sustainability and climate change. However, Lila soon realized that her feed had become an echo chamber—she only saw posts that aligned with her existing beliefs and rarely encountered different viewpoints.

To break out of this bubble, Lila started following accounts that approached environmental issues from various angles, including businesses, policymakers, and even skeptics.

At first, engaging with content that challenged her assumptions was uncomfortable, but over time, Lila found that it helped her develop a more nuanced understanding of the complex issues surrounding environmentalism.

By intentionally seeking out diverse perspectives, Lila was able to expand her horizons and engage in more productive conversations about the topics she cared about. She learned to approach activism with empathy and open-mindedness and became a more effective advocate for change.

Another key strategy is to be intentional with your attention. Just because something pops up on your screen doesn't mean you have to engage with it. Take a moment to ask yourself: Is this content adding value to my life, or is it just noise? If it's the latter, feel free to scroll on by.

 Exercise 1: The Attention Audit

To become more intentional with your attention, try conducting an attention audit. For one day, keep a log of the content you consume online. Each time you encounter a post, article, or video, ask yourself:

- Is this content informative, inspiring, or entertaining in a way that aligns with my values and goals?

- Does this content make me feel good about myself and the world around me, or does it trigger negative emotions like anxiety, anger, or FOMO?

- Is this content worth the time I'm spending on it, or could I be using this time for something more productive or fulfilling?

Keep track of your answers in a journal or notes app. At the end of the day, review your log and reflect on your digital consumption habits.

Are you happy with how you're spending your attention online, or are there areas where you'd like to make changes?

Based on your reflections, set some intentions for your future digital consumption. Maybe you want to limit your social media use to certain times of day, or perhaps you want to seek out more content that aligns with your personal growth goals. Whatever your intentions, remember that you have the power to take control of your attention and shape your digital experience.

Truth or Trash: Identifying Misinformation in Your Feed

In the digital age, misinformation spreads like wildfire. It's up to you to be the firefighter and stop it in its tracks. But how can you tell what's true and what's not? Here are a few tips:

- **Check the source:** Is the information coming from a reputable news outlet, or is it from a sketchy website you've never heard of? Look for established media brands with a track record of accuracy.

- **Be wary of sensationalism:** If a headline seems too good (or bad) to be true, it probably is. Clickbait titles often exaggerate or mislead to get your attention.

- **Cross-reference with other sources:** If you see a wild claim, do a quick search to see if other credible outlets are reporting the same thing. If it's only showing up on fringe sites, that's a red flag.

- **Use fact-checking tools like Snopes or PolitiFact to verify information:** These sites specialize in debunking false claims and can help you separate fact from fiction.

 Exercise 2: Spot the Misinformation

To sharpen your misinformation-spotting skills, try this exercise:

1. Find a piece of content online that makes a claim about a topic you're interested in. This could be a news article, social media post, or video.

2. Before reading or watching the content, make a note of the headline or main claim. Does it seem sensationalized or too good to be true?

3. As you engage with the content, pay attention to the sources cited (if any). Are they reputable? Do they have expertise on the topic?

4. After finishing the content, do a quick fact-check using the strategies outlined above. Search for other credible sources reporting on the same claim and see if the information lines up.

5. Based on your fact-checking, determine whether the content is likely to be true, false, or somewhere in between.

Note any red flags you noticed and how you arrived at your conclusion.

By practicing this exercise regularly, you'll develop a keen eye for spotting misinformation and be better equipped to navigate the digital landscape with confidence.

The Art of Selective Attention Online: What to Ignore, What to Absorb

With so much content vying for your attention, it's crucial to be selective about what you let into your brain. Think of your attention as a precious resource—you only have so much to give, so make it count.

One way to do this is by curating your follows. Take a hard look at the accounts you follow on social media and ask yourself:

Do they add value to my life, or do they just stress me out? Don't be afraid to hit that unfollow button if an account is constantly bringing you down.

 Case Study 2: Digital Decluttering for Mental Health

Marcus, a 17-year-old from New York City, was an avid gamer and spent hours each day watching livestreams and engaging with gaming communities online. At first, this hobby brought him joy and connection, but over time, Marcus started to feel overwhelmed and drained by the constant stream of content.

After some self-reflection, Marcus realized that many of the accounts he followed were fueling toxic behaviors like competitiveness, aggression, and negativity. He decided it was time for a digital declutter.

Marcus unfollowed accounts that consistently made him feel bad about himself or triggered negative emotions. He muted keywords and phrases that he found triggering or harmful. He set boundaries around his gaming time, making sure to prioritize offline activities like exercise, socializing, and schoolwork.

As a result of his digital decluttering, Marcus found that he had more energy and focus for the things that truly mattered to him. He still enjoyed gaming, but he approached it with a healthier mindset and better boundaries. By being selective about the content he consumed, Marcus was able to improve his mental health and overall well-being.

Another strategy is to set boundaries around your screen time. It's easy to fall down the rabbit hole of endless scrolling, but that's a surefire way to overwhelm your brain. Try setting specific times of day to check social media and stick to them. You can also use apps like Freedom or Forest to block distracting sites and stay focused.

When you do engage with content, be an active consumer. Don't just passively absorb whatever comes your way—think critically about the messages you're receiving. Ask yourself: Who created this content, and what is their agenda? What biases or assumptions are at play? By engaging your critical thinking skills, you can absorb information more mindfully.

Exercise 3: Digital Boundary-Setting

To create healthy boundaries around your digital consumption, try this exercise:

1. Make a list of the online activities that tend to suck you in and distract you from your goals. This could be social media, gaming, online shopping, or anything else.

2. For each activity, set a specific boundary that feels realistic and sustainable for you. For example, you might decide to limit your social media use to 30 minutes per day, or you might commit to only checking your email twice a day.

3. Write down your boundaries and post them somewhere visible, like your desk or lock screen. This will help you stay accountable and remind you of your intentions.

4. Track your progress over the course of a week. Each day, make a note of whether you stuck to your boundaries or not. If you slipped up, don't beat yourself up—just reflect on what triggered the slip-up and how you can avoid it in the future.

5. At the end of the week, reflect on how your digital boundaries affected your mood, productivity, and overall well-being. Make adjustments as needed, and keep tweaking your boundaries until you find a balance that works for you.

Remember, setting digital boundaries is a personal process, and what works for one person may not work for another.

The key is to be intentional and mindful about your consumption and to prioritize your mental health and well-being above all else.

Building Your Digital Literacy: Tools Every Teen Should Know

To navigate the digital world effectively, you need the right tools in your tool kit. Here are a few essential skills every teen should master:

First up: search skills. Knowing how to find reliable information online is a superpower. Start by using reputable search engines like Google Scholar or JSTOR for academic research. For general queries, try advanced search techniques like using quotation marks around a phrase to find exact matches or using the minus sign to exclude certain words.

 Exercise 4: The Google Scholar Challenge

To level up your academic search skills, try the Google Scholar Challenge:

1. Pick a topic you're curious about or need to research for a school project. It could be anything from the history of video games to the science of climate change.

2. Open up Google Scholar, a freely accessible web search engine (scholar.google.com) that indexes the full text or metadata of scholarly literature across an array of publishing formats and disciplines. It provides a simple way to broadly search for scholarly articles, theses, books, and conference papers, offering features like citation counts and related articles to facilitate academic research.

3. Do a quick search for your topic. Scan the results and take note of the types of sources that come up (e.g., journal articles, conference papers, books).

4. Refine your search by adding more specific keywords or using advanced search techniques like quotation marks or Boolean operators (AND, OR, NOT). See how the results change based on your search terms.

5. Choose a few promising sources and read through the abstracts or summaries. Note the key findings or arguments and jot down any new keywords or concepts you come across.

6. Use the "Cited by" feature to find other sources that have referenced the ones you're reading. This can be a great way to discover related research and expand your understanding of the topic.

7. Keep refining your search and reading through sources until you feel like you have a solid grasp of the current state of research on your topic. Make a note of any gaps or questions that remain unanswered—these could be areas for further exploration!

By practicing your Google Scholar skills, you'll become a more efficient and effective researcher, able to find reliable information on any topic under the sun.

Next, let's discuss privacy and security. In the age of data breaches and identity theft, it's crucial to protect your personal information online. Use strong, unique passwords for each of your accounts and enable two-factor authentication whenever possible. Be cautious about what information you share publicly on social media and adjust your privacy settings to control who can see your posts.

 ## Case Study 3: Safeguarding Your Online Reputation

Jasmine, a 19-year-old college student, had always been careful about her online presence. She kept her social media accounts private and was cautious about what she posted.

However, when she started applying for internships, she realized that her online reputation mattered more than ever.

To safeguard her reputation, Jasmine took a few key steps:

1. She Googled herself to see what came up. She found a few old posts and photos that she felt didn't represent her in the best light,

so she deleted them or adjusted her privacy settings to make them harder to find.

2. She reviewed her privacy settings on all her social media accounts and made sure that only her friends and followers could see her posts. She also turned off public search visibility so that her profiles wouldn't come up in Google searches.

3. She created a professional website and LinkedIn profile to showcase her skills and accomplishments. She made sure to use a clear, professional headshot and to highlight her relevant experience and coursework.

4. She set up Google Alerts for her name so that she would be notified if anyone posted about her online. This way, she could stay on top of her online reputation and address any negative content quickly.

By taking these proactive steps, Jasmine was able to present a polished and professional online presence to potential employers. She landed a competitive internship and felt confident that her online reputation would be an asset, not a liability, as she started her career.

Finally, don't forget about digital etiquette—aka how to be a decent human online. Treat others with respect, even if you disagree with them. Think before you post, and remember that everything you put online can potentially stay there forever. If you wouldn't say it to someone's face, don't say it online.

Exercise 5: The Empathy Experiment

To practice digital etiquette and build empathy online, try this experiment:

1. Choose a topic you feel strongly about that tends to spark heated online debates. It could be anything from politics to religion to the best pizza toppings.

2. Find an online forum or social media thread where people are discussing this topic. Choose one that has a diversity of viewpoints represented.

3. Read through the comments and try to put yourself in the shoes of each person posting. What experiences or beliefs might be shaping their perspective? What emotions might they be feeling as they engage in the debate?

4. Instead of jumping in with your own opinion, try posting a comment that acknowledges and validates someone else's perspective. Use phrases like "I can see where you're coming from" or "That's a valid point, and here's another way to look at it."

5. Notice how the tone of the conversation shifts when you approach it with empathy and respect. Do people seem more open to listening and learning from each other? Do you find yourself feeling more curious and less defensive?

By practicing empathy and etiquette online, you can help create a more positive and productive digital space for everyone.

Remember, behind every screen name and avatar is a real person with real feelings and experiences. Treat them with the same kindness and respect you would want for yourself.

The Power of Pause: Thinking Before You Share or Believe

In the fast-paced world of social media, it's easy to get caught up in the heat of the moment and react without thinking. But here's the thing: Taking a beat to pause and reflect can make a world of difference.

Before you hit that share button, ask yourself: Is this content adding value, or is it just contributing to the noise? Is it factual, or is it spreading misinformation? Is it kind, or is it hurtful? Taking a moment to consider these questions can help you make more mindful choices about what you amplify.

 ### Case Study 4: The Perils of Virtue Signaling

Aiden, a 15-year-old activist, was passionate about social justice and spent a lot of time engaging with political content online. He often felt pressure to react quickly to breaking news and to show his support for various causes by sharing posts and memes.

One day, Aiden came across a viral video that claimed to show a police officer using excessive force against a peaceful protester. Without pausing to fact-check or consider the full context, Aiden shared the video on his social media accounts, adding a caption expressing his outrage and calls for action.

However, it later emerged that the video had been heavily edited and taken out of context. The full footage showed that the protester had actually been the aggressor and that the officer had used reasonable force to defend himself and others.

Aiden was mortified that he had contributed to the spread of misinformation and potentially damaged an innocent person's reputation.

He realized that he had failed to think critically and act responsibly in his rush to signal his virtue and align himself with a cause.

From that day forward, Aiden committed to pausing and reflecting before sharing any content online. He took the time to fact-check claims, consider multiple perspectives, and ask himself whether his posts truly added value to the conversation. As a result, he became a more effective and respected activist, able to build bridges and create positive change both online and off.

The same goes for forming opinions. It's easy to see a compelling headline or a persuasive tweet and immediately accept it as truth. But the reality is often more complex. Before you adopt a new belief, take the time to research and consider multiple perspectives. Seek out credible sources and look for evidence to support claims. You can build a more nuanced understanding of the world by thinking critically and resisting knee-jerk reactions

 Exercise 6: The Opinion Audit

To become more mindful of how you form opinions and beliefs, try this audit exercise:

1. Make a list of 5–10 opinions or beliefs you hold strongly. These could be related to politics, religion, social issues, or anything else.

2. For each opinion, ask yourself: Where did this belief come from? Did I inherit it from my family or community? Did I arrive at it through my own research and reflection, or did I absorb it from the media or social media?

3. Next, consider the evidence you have to support each belief. Have you sought out multiple credible sources? Have you considered counterarguments or alternative perspectives? Or are you relying on anecdotal evidence or gut feelings?

4. Commit to doing further research for any beliefs that feel shaky or unsupported. Seek out reputable sources and experts, and be open to changing your mind if the evidence points in a different direction.

5. Moving forward, make a habit of pausing and reflecting before forming opinions on complex topics. Train yourself to seek out diverse perspectives and to approach new ideas with curiosity rather than knee-jerk skepticism or acceptance. By building this habit of critical thinking, you'll be better equipped to navigate the ever-changing landscape of the digital age.

Curating Your Digital Diet: Feeding Your Mind Healthy Content

Navigating the online world can sometimes feel like trying to drink from a firehose. There's just so much information coming at you from every direction, and it's easy to get overwhelmed and lost in the noise.

But here's the good news: You have the power to curate your own digital experience. Just like you wouldn't eat junk food all day, every day (okay, maybe sometimes, but you get the point), you shouldn't fill your brain with digital junk either.

So, how do you create a healthy, balanced digital diet? It all starts with being intentional about the content you consume. Instead of mindlessly scrolling through your feeds, take a step back and think about what truly lights you up and makes you feel good. Is it learning about new cultures and perspectives? Geeking out over the latest sci-fi novels? Connecting with friends and family who make you laugh until your face hurts?

Exercise 7: The Digital Diet Plan

But here's the thing: Curating a healthy digital diet isn't just about what you consume but also how you consume it.

Just like you wouldn't scarf down a whole pizza in one sitting (again, no judgment), you shouldn't binge on digital content. Set some boundaries for yourself and create a routine that feels sustainable and nourishing.

Maybe that means dedicating a certain amount of time each day to reading articles from your favorite websites or listening to podcasts while you go for a walk. Maybe it means keeping a journal where you jot down your thoughts and reactions to the content you consume. The key is finding a rhythm that works for you and leaves you feeling energized and inspired, not drained and overwhelmed.

And remember, your digital diet isn't set in stone. Just like your taste buds change over time, so will your digital preferences. Don't be afraid to mix things up and seek out new voices and perspectives. The goal is to create a dynamic, ever-evolving diet that keeps your mind nourished and engaged.

Here's a step-by-step exercise to help you curate a healthy digital diet:

1. **Audit your current digital consumption:**

    - Make a list of all the digital content you consume regularly, including social media, websites, podcasts, and videos.

    - Note how much time you spend on each platform or type of content.

- Reflect on how each type of content makes you feel after consuming it.

Curating a healthy digital diet is an ongoing process that requires self-awareness, intention, and flexibility. By following these steps and staying committed to your goals, you can create a digital consumption plan that nourishes your mind and enhances your overall well-being.

1 – Set clear goals for your digital diet:

- Determine what you want to achieve through your digital consumption (e.g., learning, entertainment, personal growth).
- Identify the types of content that align with your goals and values.
- Prioritize the content that brings you the most value and satisfaction.

2 – Create a sustainable routine:

- Allocate specific times throughout the day for consuming digital content, such as dedicating 30 minutes in the morning to reading articles or listening to podcasts during your lunch break.
- Establish boundaries by setting time limits for each session to avoid overdoing it.
- Be mindful of your digital consumption and avoid multitasking while engaging with content.

3 – Engage actively with the content:

- Take notes or summarize key points from the articles or podcasts you consume.

- Keep a journal to jot down your thoughts, ideas, and reactions to the content.

- Discuss the content with others to gain new perspectives and deepen your understanding.

4 – Regularly reassess and adjust your digital diet:

- Review your digital consumption habits every few weeks and evaluate whether they align with your goals.

- Don't hesitate to unfollow or unsubscribe from sources that no longer serve you or align with your values.

- Seek out new sources of content that challenge your thinking and expand your knowledge.

5 – Practice digital mindfulness:

- Before consuming any digital content, take a moment to check in with yourself and ask whether it aligns with your goals and values.

- After consuming content, reflect on how it made you feel and whether it was worth your time and attention.

- Be intentional about the content you share and engage with online, ensuring that it contributes positively to your digital environment.

 Case Study 5: Bursting the Filter Bubble

Curating a healthy digital diet isn't just about you. It's also about the kind of digital world you want to help create. Every time you like, share, or comment on a post, you're adding your voice to the conversation. Every time you amplify a marginalized perspective or stand up against misinformation, you're helping to shape the digital landscape for the better.

So, as you go forth and conquer the digital world, keep in mind the kind of legacy you want to leave behind. Do you want to be known as the person who always shared the latest gossip and drama, or do you want to be remembered as someone who used their platform to make a real difference?

The choice is yours, my friend. You have the power to shape your digital reality and to help create a more informed, empathetic, and just world. So, go ahead and make your mark—the internet is waiting for you.

Putting It All Together

If you ever feel lost or overwhelmed along the way, just remember: You're not alone. Reach out to your friends, family, and mentors for guidance and support. Lean on the communities that lift you up and make you feel seen and heard. Together, we can navigate this wild, wonderful, and sometimes wacky digital landscape and come out the other side stronger, wiser, and more connected than ever before.

So, what are you waiting for? Go forth and curate the heck out of your digital diet. Your brain (and the world) will thank you.

Chapter 2

Enhancing Emotional Intelligence in the Digital Realm

"Connect to the world through your screen but remember to tune into your emotions. The truest connection starts within." -- LLR Academy

In the last chapter, we talked about how to curate a healthy, nourishing digital diet that feeds your mind and soul. But as any savvy internet user knows, thriving in the digital world takes more than just consuming the right content. It also requires a special set of skills and mindsets we like to call "digital emotional intelligence."

What exactly is digital emotional intelligence, you ask? Simply put, it's the ability to recognize, understand, and manage your own emotions—as well as the emotions of others —in a digital context. It's about being able to express yourself authentically and empathetically online while also setting healthy boundaries and staying grounded in the face of digital drama.

In this chapter, we'll dive deep into the world of digital emotional intelligence and explore some practical strategies for cultivating it in your own life. From mastering the art of the emoji to navigating the treacherous waters of social media comparison, we've got you covered. So, take a deep breath, put on your favorite playlist, and let's get emotionally intelligent together!

Emojis and Emotions: Expressing Feelings in a Digital World

Let's start with one of the most ubiquitous tools in the digital emotional intelligence tool kit: the humble emoji. Whether you're a fan of the classic smiley face or prefer the more expressive options like the dancing lady or the eggplant (hey, we don't judge), there's no denying that emojis have become an essential part of our online communication.

But here's the thing: Emojis aren't just cute little pictures we use to decorate our messages. They actually serve a really important function when it comes to expressing our emotions in a digital world. When we communicate face to face, we rely on things like facial expressions, tone of voice, and body language to convey our feelings and intentions.

But when we communicate through a screen, those nonverbal cues get lost in translation.

That's where emojis come in. Adding a well-placed smiley face or heart icon to our messages can help bridge the gap between what we're saying and how we're feeling. Emojis allow us to add an extra layer of emotional context to our words, making it easier for others to understand and relate to us.

Of course, like any tool, emojis can be misused or overused. We've all seen those messages that are more emoji than text or the dreaded "emoji only" response that leaves us wondering what the heck the other person is trying to say. So, while emojis can be a powerful way to express ourselves emotionally online, it's important to use them judiciously and in combination with clear, direct communication.

 Exercise 8: Emoji Translator

Think of a common phrase or sentiment you might express online, like "I'm so excited for the weekend!" or "I'm really stressed out about this project." Now, try to translate that phrase into emojis only.

See how many different ways you can express the same sentiment using only emojis. Then, try using your emoji translations in a real conversation with a friend or family member. Notice how the emojis change the tone and feel of the message and how your conversation partner responds.

By getting creative with your emoji use and paying attention to how others interpret them, you can start to build your digital emotional intelligence muscles and become a more expressive, empathetic communicator online.

Digital Empathy: Understanding Emotions Behind the Screen

Speaking of empathy, let's talk about one of the most important skills in the digital emotional intelligence tool kit: the ability to understand and share the feelings of others, even when you can't see them face to face.

It's easy to forget sometimes that behind every screen name and avatar, there's a real human being with real emotions, experiences, and struggles. When we communicate online, it can be tempting to project our own assumptions and biases onto others or to get caught up in the heat of the moment and say things we might regret later.

But just like in real life, empathy is key to building strong, healthy relationships online. When we take the time to put ourselves in others' shoes and try to understand where they're coming from, we open up the possibility for deeper connection, understanding, and compassion.

So, how can you cultivate digital empathy in your own life? Here are a few tips:

- **Practice active listening:** When you're reading someone's message or post, really try to hear what they're saying beyond just the words on the screen. Pay attention to the emotions and experiences they're sharing and try to imagine how you might feel in their situation.

- **Ask clarifying questions:** If something someone says online confuses you or rubs you the wrong way, don't just react impulsively. Take a moment to ask clarifying questions and try to understand their perspective better. You might be surprised by what you learn!

- **Use "I" statements:** When expressing your own feelings or opinions online, try to use "I" statements that focus on your own experiences and emotions, rather than making accusations or assumptions about others. For example, instead of saying "You always do this," try saying "I feel frustrated when this happens."

- **Remember the human:** At the end of the day, the people you interact with online are just that—people. They have hopes, fears, dreams, and struggles just like you do. Try to approach your online interactions with the same kind of respect, kindness, and empathy you would want to be treated with in person.

 Case Study 5: The Social Media Misunderstanding

Scarlet and Tanya have been friends since childhood, but their relationship has been strained lately. It all started with a misunderstanding on social media.

Scarlet had posted a vague, cryptic message about feeling betrayed and let down by someone close to her. Tanya, scrolling through her feed late at night, saw the post and immediately assumed it was about her. She fired off an angry, defensive comment accusing Scarlet of being passive-aggressive and attention-seeking.

The comment sparked a heated back-and-forth between the two friends, with each one becoming more and more entrenched in their own perspective. The argument quickly spiraled out of control, with both Scarlet and Tanya saying hurtful things they didn't really mean.

Finally, after a few days of radio silence, Scarlet reached out to Tanya with a heartfelt message. She apologized for being vague in her original post and explained that it had actually been about a situation at work, not their friendship. She asked Tanya if they could talk on the phone and clear the air.

Tanya, reading Scarlet's message with fresh eyes, felt a wave of regret wash over her. She realized that she had let her own insecurities and assumptions cloud her judgment and had reacted impulsively instead of trying to understand Scarlet's perspective. She agreed to the phone call and apologized for her part in the misunderstanding.

As the two friends talked, they were able to see the situation from each other's point of view and find a way forward. They agreed to be more direct and honest with each other in the future and to always assume the best intentions behind each other's words and actions.

The social media misunderstanding had been painful for both Scarlet and Tanya, but it had also taught them a valuable lesson about the importance of digital empathy. By taking the time to listen, clarify, and put themselves in each other's shoes, they were able to turn a moment of conflict into an opportunity for growth and connection.

Navigating Digital Drama: Staying Calm and Collected

Let's be real: The internet can be a drama magnet. From heated comment section debates to subtweet shade to full-blown Twitter wars, it seems like there's always some kind of digital beef brewing.

But here's the thing: Getting sucked into online drama is rarely productive or fulfilling. In fact, it can be downright toxic, leaving us feeling angry, anxious, and emotionally drained.

So, how can you stay calm and collected in the face of digital drama? Here are a few strategies:

1. **Take a deep breath:** When you feel yourself getting riled up by

something you see online, take a moment to pause and breathe deeply. Close your eyes, count to ten, and focus on the sensation of the breath moving in and out of your body. This simple act of mindfulness can help you regain your center and respond from a place of clarity and intention, rather than reactivity.

2. **Get curious:** Instead of immediately jumping to conclusions or attacking the other person, get curious about their perspective. Ask yourself: what might be motivating them to say or do this? What experiences or beliefs might be shaping their point of view? By approaching the situation with curiosity instead of judgment, you open up the possibility for deeper understanding and connection.

3. **Know when to walk away:** Sometimes, no matter how much empathy and curiosity you bring to the table, a situation is simply too toxic or unproductive to engage with. In those cases, it's okay to walk away and disengage. You don't have to attend every argument you're invited to!

4. **Find healthy outlets:** When digital drama starts to get under your skin, it's important to have healthy outlets for processing your emotions. Whether it's journaling, talking to a trusted friend, or going for a run, find activities that help you release stress and maintain your emotional equilibrium.

 Exercise 9: The Drama Detox

Think of a recent online interaction that left you feeling triggered, angry, or defensive. Now, imagine that you could go back in time and respond to that situation differently.

Take a few deep breaths and really put yourself in that moment. What were you feeling when you first saw the triggering content? What thoughts were running through your head?

Now, imagine hitting the pause button on your initial reaction. Instead of responding impulsively, take a moment to get curious about the other person's perspective. What questions could you ask to better understand where they're coming from?

If the situation still feels toxic or unproductive after attempting to engage with empathy and curiosity, imagine yourself calmly and firmly disengaging. What would you say to the other person to set a boundary and protect your emotional well-being?

Finally, imagine yourself taking some time to process your emotions in a healthy way after the interaction. What activities or practices would help you release any residual stress or negativity?

By mentally rehearsing these steps, you can train your brain to respond to digital drama with greater calm, clarity, and intentionality. The more you practice, the more natural it will start to feel in real-life situations.

The Balance Between Online Connection and Emotional Detachment

As much as we may love the thrill of a good group chat or the rush of likes on our latest Instagram post, it's important to remember that online connection is not the same as in-person connection. While digital tools can be amazing for staying in touch with friends and loved ones, building communities around shared interests, and expanding our horizons, they can also create a sense of emotional detachment if we're not careful.

Think about it: When we communicate through a screen, it's easy to forget that there's a real, live human on the other end. We might say things we would never say to someone's face or get so caught up in crafting the perfect post that we lose sight of our authentic selves.

So, how can you strike a balance between online connection and emotional detachment? Here are a few ideas:

- **Prioritize face-to-face interactions:** As much as possible, make time for in-person connection with the people you care about. Whether it's a coffee date with a friend or a family dinner, there's no substitute for the depth and richness of face-to-face interaction.

- **Set boundaries around screen time:** While staying connected online is great, it's also important to have times of the day or week when you unplug and focus on the present moment. Consider setting specific "no-screen zones" in your home or creating rituals around device-free time, like a weekly digital detox day.

- **Be mindful of your online persona:** When you're posting or interacting online, take a moment to check in with yourself: Is this an authentic representation of who I am and what I value? Am I presenting myself in a way that feels true and aligned, or am I getting caught up in the performance of it all?

- **Cultivate offline hobbies and interests:** Make sure you have plenty of offline activities and pursuits that bring you joy, fulfillment, and a sense of purpose. Whether it's playing an instrument, exploring nature, or volunteering for a cause you care about, having a rich offline life can help you keep your online life in perspective.

Case Study 6: The Instagram Infatuation

Liam had always been a bit of a shy, introverted guy, but when he discovered Instagram, it was like a whole new world opened up. He loved scrolling through his feed, seeing what his friends and acquaintances were up to, and posting his own carefully curated photos and captions.

At first, Instagram felt like a fun, harmless way for Liam to connect with others and express himself creatively.

But as time went on, Liam found himself becoming more and more obsessed with his online persona. He would spend hours editing his photos, agonizing over the perfect caption, and refreshing his notifications to see how many likes and comments he had received.

Liam's Instagram infatuation started to take a toll on his real-life relationships and responsibilities. He would cancel plans with friends to stay home and work on his feed, and he began to feel anxious and depressed when his posts didn't get as much engagement as he had hoped.

One day, after a particularly low-engagement post sent Liam into a spiral of self-doubt and negativity, he decided enough was enough. He realized that he had become too emotionally attached to his online persona and that it was time to take a step back and reevaluate his relationship with social media.

Liam started by setting some boundaries around his Instagram use. He committed to checking the app only once a day and spending no more than 30 minutes on it at a time. He also made a list of offline activities and hobbies he wanted to prioritize, like playing guitar and going on hikes with friends.

As Liam started to cultivate a more balanced and authentic life both on and offline, he found that his relationship with Instagram started to shift. He still enjoyed using the app to connect with others and express himself creatively, but it no longer held the same emotional power over him. He was able to engage with it in a way that felt healthy, intentional, and true to himself.

Liam's story is a powerful reminder of the importance of striking a balance between online connection and emotional detachment.

By setting boundaries, cultivating offline interests, and staying true to ourselves, we can enjoy the benefits of digital connection without losing sight of what really matters.

Cultivating Self-Awareness in a World of Selfies

In a world where our every move can be documented and shared online, it's easy to get caught up in the performance of it all. We might find ourselves constantly thinking about how we look, what we're doing, and how it will be perceived by others. But this constant performance can take a toll on our emotional well-being and sense of self.

That's where self-awareness comes in. Self-awareness is the ability to see ourselves clearly—our thoughts, feelings, strengths, weaknesses, and patterns of behavior. It's about being honest with ourselves about who we are and what we want and making choices that align with our values and goals.

But how can we cultivate self-awareness in a world of constant digital distraction and performance pressure? Here are a few ideas:

Practice mindfulness: Mindfulness is the practice of being present and aware in the moment, without judgment. By taking time each day to tune into your breath, your body, and your surroundings, you can start to cultivate a deeper sense of self-awareness and inner calm.

Keep a journal: Writing down your thoughts and feelings can be a powerful way to process your experiences, gain insight into your patterns and motivations, and set intentions for the future. Consider keeping a daily journal where you reflect on your day, your goals, and your emotional state.

Seek feedback from others: While it's important to trust your instincts and inner wisdom, sometimes you need an outside perspective to help you see yourself more clearly.

Consider seeking feedback from trusted friends, family members, or mentors who can offer honest, constructive insights into your strengths and areas for growth.

Question your assumptions: When you find yourself making assumptions about yourself or others, take a moment to question them. Are these assumptions based on facts, or are they just stories you've been telling yourself? By challenging your assumptions and looking at situations from multiple angles, you can start to cultivate a more flexible, open-minded sense of self.

 Exercise 10: The Self-Reflection Selfie

1 - The next time you find yourself reaching for your phone to take a selfie, try this instead:

Take a moment to pause and tune into your breath. Notice the sensation of the air moving in and out of your body and feel your feet planted firmly on the ground.

2 – Now, instead of taking a photo of your external appearance, take an internal "selfie" of your emotional state. Ask yourself:

- What am I feeling in this moment?

- What thoughts are running through my head?

- What are my intentions for taking this selfie?

- How do I want to show up in the world today?

3 – Take a few minutes to journal or reflect on your answers to these questions. Consider setting an intention for how you want to show up online today. Maybe it's to post something authentic and vulnerable or to engage with others from a place of curiosity and compassion. Whatever your intention, let it guide your actions and interactions throughout the day.

By taking a moment to pause and reflect before engaging with social media, you can start to cultivate a deeper sense of self-awareness and intentionality in your online life. And who knows? You might just inspire others to do the same!

From Comparison to Compassion: Overcoming Social Media Envy

Let's face it: Social media can be a breeding ground for comparison and envy. We scroll through our feeds and see people who seem to have it all—the perfect body, the dream job, the lavish lifestyle—and it's easy to start feeling like we don't measure up.

But remember: Comparison is the thief of joy. When we get caught up in comparing ourselves to others, we lose sight of our unique strengths, talents, and blessings. We start to feel like we're not enough, and that can lead to feelings of anxiety, depression, and low self-worth.

So, how can we move from comparison to compassion in our online lives? Here are a few ideas:

- **Remember that social media is a highlight reel:** People tend to post their best moments and accomplishments on social media, not their struggles and setbacks. When you find yourself comparing your behind-the-scenes to someone else's highlight reel, remember that you're not seeing the full picture.

- **Celebrate others' successes:** Instead of feeling envious of others' accomplishments, try to cultivate a sense of joy and celebration for them. Remember that someone else's success doesn't diminish your own and that there's enough abundance and opportunity in the world for everyone.

- **Practice gratitude:** When you find yourself slipping into comparison mode, take a moment to focus on the things you're grateful for in your own life. Maybe it's your health, your relationships, your talents, or your personal growth. By shifting your focus to gratitude, you can start to cultivate a more positive, abundant mindset.

- **Unfollow accounts that trigger you:** If certain accounts or people consistently make you feel bad about yourself, consider unfollowing or muting them. You don't need that kind of negativity in your life!

 Case Study 7: The Green-Eyed Monster

Sasha had always been a confident, ambitious person, but lately she had been feeling more and more insecure. It seemed like everywhere she looked on social media, people were achieving amazing things—landing dream jobs, traveling the world, getting engaged to their soulmates.

At first, Sasha tried to use these posts as motivation to work harder and achieve more in her own life. But the more she scrolled, the more inadequate she felt. She started to compare herself to others in every area of her life, from her career to her relationships to her physical appearance.

One day, after a particularly triggering scroll session, Sasha decided enough was enough. She realized that her comparison habit was only making her feel worse about herself and that it was time to make a change.

Sasha started by unfollowing some of the accounts that consistently made her feel bad about herself. She also made a list of things she was grateful for in her own life, like her supportive family, her thriving freelance business, and her passion for photography.

Whenever Sasha caught herself slipping into comparison mode, she would take a deep breath and focus on one of the things on her gratitude list. She also started making an effort to celebrate others' successes instead of feeling threatened by them.

Over time, Sasha started to notice a shift in her mindset. Instead of feeling envious and inadequate when she saw others achieving great things, she felt inspired and motivated.

She started to see others' successes as proof that anything was possible, and she began to focus on her unique path and purpose.

By moving from comparison to compassion, Sasha was able to cultivate a more positive, abundant mindset both online and off. She still had moments of insecurity and self-doubt, but she was better equipped to handle them with grace and self-compassion.

Sasha's story is a powerful reminder that we all have a choice in how we engage with social media. By choosing compassion over comparison, we can create a more supportive, uplifting digital culture for ourselves and others.

Wrap-up

And there you have it, folks—a whirlwind tour of emotional intelligence in the digital age! We've covered a lot of ground in this chapter, from the power of emojis to the perils of social media envy. But at the end of the day, it all comes down to one thing: being intentional about how we show up online.

When we approach our digital lives with self-awareness, empathy, and compassion, we create a ripple effect of positivity that can touch countless others. We become a force for good in a world that can often feel chaotic and overwhelming.

So, go forth and spread those good vibes, my friends! Use your emojis wisely, engage with curiosity and kindness, and remember that your online presence is a reflection of your deepest values and truest self.

And if you ever find yourself getting caught up in the drama or the comparison trap, take a deep breath and remember: You've got this. You have the power to create the digital world you want to see, one post, one comment, one heart at a time.

Thanks for joining me on this journey into the wild and wonderful world of digital emotional intelligence. I hope you've learned a thing or two, and more importantly, I hope you've had some fun along the way.

Chapter 3

Mastering Time Management and Productivity

"Your time is your canvas; paint it with purpose. Make every moment count toward crafting the masterpiece of your life."
– LLR Academy

Imagine you're juggling three balls named School, Social Media, and Sleep. Dropping any of them isn't an option, right? Welcome to the daily grind of life where balancing academics, scrolling through TikTok, and getting decent shuteye feels like a circus act. But what if I told you there's a way to keep all balls in the air without breaking a sweat? It's all about mastering the art of time management and productivity in our hyper-connected world. This chapter is your guide to becoming a pro juggler, ensuring that none of your essential balls hit the ground.

Balancing Acts: Juggling School, Social Media, and Sleep

First things first, let's talk priorities. It's easy to let social media sneak up on your priority list—after all, that quick check on Instagram can suddenly morph into an hour-long dive. But here's the kicker: When schoolwork and sleep fall behind in your list of priorities, everything else starts to crumble. You know the drill—cramming for tests, pulling all-nighters, and feeling like a zombie the next day.

So, how do you keep your academics and well-being from getting sideswiped by your social feed? It starts with a conscious decision to prioritize. Think of your energy as a budget. How much do you want to spend on different activities? Put academics and sleep at the top of your budget list. This doesn't mean you cut out social media—instead, you manage it so it doesn't encroach on your essentials. Setting specific times for study and rest—and sticking to them—can help you manage your day efficiently without missing out on the fun stuff.

Now, crafting a balanced schedule might sound about as fun as watching paint dry, but hear me out—it can be a game changer. Start with the non-negotiables: school hours and sleep. These set the framework of your daily schedule. Next, block out dedicated study times. These should be times when you're typically most alert and productive—right after school or maybe after dinner, depending on your rhythm.

With the essentials penciled in, you can see how much time is left for other activities like social media, hanging out with friends, or hobbies. Here's where you can get creative. Maybe you decide to check social media for a few minutes after completing a study session as a reward. Or, perhaps you schedule a 20-minute social media break before starting homework to clear your head. The key is making sure these breaks are deliberate and timed. The Pomodoro Technique—working for 25 minutes and breaking for 5 minutes—is perfect for this. It keeps you refreshed without letting breaks overrun your productivity

 Case Study 8: The Social Media Spiral

Maria, a high school sophomore, found herself struggling to keep up with her schoolwork and sleep schedule. She would often find herself scrolling through social media late into the night, telling herself, "Just five more minutes." Those minutes would turn into hours, and before she knew it, it was 2 a.m. and she had barely started her homework. The next day, exhausted and groggy, Maria would struggle to focus on class, and her grades started to slip.

Recognizing the problem, Maria decided to make a change. She set specific times for studying and sleeping and stuck to them rigidly. She also allocated a 30-minute slot each day for social media right after her study sessions as a reward. By prioritizing her essentials and treating social media as a limited treat rather than an unlimited indulgence, Maria found she was able to enjoy her online interactions more while also excelling in school and feeling well-rested

The Myth of Multitasking: Focusing on a Tab-Open World

Let's bust a myth you've probably held onto for a long time: multitasking. It sounds cool, right? Like you're a super-efficient robot tackling multiple things at once.

Only, science tells us it's more like trying to run in different directions simultaneously—you don't really get far. Studies reveal that what we think of as multitasking is actually task-switching, and it's not doing us any favors (Miller, n.d.). Every time you switch from typing an essay to checking a text or a tweet, your brain has to reorient itself. This constant shift not only slows you down but also drains mental energy, making you less productive and more prone to errors.

Evidence stacks up, showing that juggling tasks can increase stress and decrease productivity. According to research from Stanford University, heavy multitaskers are less competent at distinguishing relevant from irrelevant details, and they find it harder to switch between tasks compared to those who complete one task at a time (Gorlick, 2016). So, if multitasking isn't the productivity booster it's cracked up to be, what's the alternative? Enter unitasking, a fancy term for doing one thing at a time, which might just be your ticket to better grades and less burnout.

The magic of focusing on one task at a time can't be overstated. When you unitask, you give whatever you're doing—whether it's a calculus problem or a creative writing assignment—your full attention. This focus can lead to better work quality, quicker completion, and a deeper understanding of the material. Think of it as being fully present with your task, similar to how you'd listen intently to a friend without distractions.

Exercise 11: The Single-Tab Challenge

For one day, every time you need to focus on a task, whether it's studying, writing an essay, or researching for a project, challenge yourself to keep only one tab open in your browser. If you need to look something up, close the extra tab as soon as you've found the information you need. Notice how this affects your focus and productivity compared to your usual multi-tab browsing. Do you find yourself less distracted and able to dive deeper into your work?

If the single-tab method works well for you, try extending the challenge to a week and see how it impacts your overall efficiency and output.

Digital Tools That Truly Enhance Your Productivity

Let's face it: The right tools can make or break your productivity game. Think about it like this: You wouldn't try to hammer a nail using a screwdriver, right? Similarly, tackling your academic and personal tasks with the right digital tools can mean the difference between smashing your goals and simply scraping by. Finding the perfect fit for your needs in this age of apps and digital solutions can seem overwhelming, but getting it right can seriously turbocharge your efficiency. So, let's dive into some stellar productivity apps, customize them to suit your style, and explore how other digital tools like time management software and digital calendars can keep you on top of your game.

Starting with productivity apps, these digital buddies can be your best allies in managing your hectic life. Whether it's keeping track of your assignments, managing your time, or even blocking out distractions, there's an app out there that can help. For example, Trello is fantastic for visual planners. It allows you to organize your projects into boards, lists, and cards where you can track progress, set deadlines, and even collaborate with classmates or group project members. It's like having a digital bulletin board that's both fun and functional.

Then, there's Evernote, a versatile app perfect for students who need to jot down everything from lecture notes to those midnight brainwaves. What sets Evernote apart is its ability to sync across all your devices, so you can switch from your laptop during class to reviewing notes on your phone during a bus ride home without missing a beat. Plus, you can attach PDFs, save web pages, and even search handwritten notes. For those who find themselves frequently off-track, apps like Forest offer a creative solution.

This app helps you focus by growing a virtual tree that flourishes as you work but withers if you leave the app to check Instagram or Snapchat. It's a visually rewarding way to keep yourself disciplined!

 Case Study 9: The App-Powered Project

Kai was working on a big science project with a group from his class. With each member responsible for different sections and everyone on different schedules, coordination was a nightmare. Kai decided to take the lead and introduced his team to Trello. He set up a board for the project, with lists for each section and cards for each task. The team used the app to assign tasks, set deadlines, and collaborate on research and writing. They attached relevant files and links to each card, making all the information they needed readily accessible.

Thanks to Trello's visual organization and easy collaboration, Kai's team sailed through the project. They could see at a glance what needed to be done, who was responsible for what, and how close they were to completion. The app streamlined their teamwork and communication, leading to a top-grade project and a newfound appreciation for the power of digital tools.

Creating a Productive Study Space in the Digital Age

When it comes to hitting the books and really getting into the zone, your environment can make or break your study vibe. Think about it: You wouldn't try to sleep in a nightclub or work out in a library, right? Each activity thrives in its tailored environment. So, let's design a digital study zone that not only looks cool but actually tricks your brain into wanting to study.

Creating a physical and digital environment conducive to focused study starts with understanding what elements distract you and what helps you focus.
Start with the physical setup. Find a quiet corner in your home where you can set up a dedicated study space—no dual-purposing your bed or couch. A clear, designated area signals your brain that it's time to switch gears from relaxation to work mode. Next, think about what you need within arm's reach. Have all your study materials handy: textbooks, notebooks, pens, and maybe a water bottle to stay hydrated. Clutter is a no-go; it's not just a distraction but can actually cause stress and hinder your ability to focus.

Now, turn your attention to the digital environment on your computer or tablet. Organize your digital desktop as carefully as your physical one. Create specific folders for each subject or project and keep all relevant files there—no more desktop full of random documents and screenshots. Use bookmarks smartly in your web browser to keep essential educational resources just a click away. Also, consider the aesthetics of your digital workspace. A pleasing wallpaper, a simple, clean interface, and organized files can make your digital study zone inviting and stimulating.

Exercise 12: The Study Space Makeover

Take a critical look at your current study space, both physical and digital. Make a list of the elements that are helping you focus and those that are hindering your concentration. Do you have unnecessary clutter on your desk or distracting posters on the wall? Is your computer desktop a jumble of random files and folders? Follow these directions to give your study space a makeover:

1 – Assessment Phase

- Take a critical look at your current study space, both physical and digital.

- List elements helping you focus and those hindering your concentration.

- Identify unnecessary clutter on your desk or distracting items in your space.

- Evaluate your computer desktop for organization and distractions.

2 – Preparation Phase

- Set aside 1–2 hours for the study space makeover

- Gather supplies like storage bins, organizers, and cleaning tools.

- Prepare mentally by envisioning your ideal study space.

3 – Physical Space Makeover

- Clear away unnecessary items from your desk and the surrounding area.

- Organize what's left in a functional and visually pleasing manner.

- Consider adding plants or décor that promote a calm and focused atmosphere.

4 – Digital Space Makeover

- Create a folder system for your classes and projects.

- Clear your computer desktop of any unnecessary files.

- Choose a calming wallpaper that isn't visually distracting.

5 – Testing and Adjustment

- Study in your new setup for at least an hour.

- Note how the changes affect your ability to concentrate.

- Make further adjustments if needed based on your experience.

6 – Reflection

- Reflect on the overall effectiveness of your study space makeover.

- Consider what worked well and what could be improved for future setups.

- Celebrate your efforts in creating a more conducive study environment.

Time-Blocking Techniques for the Busy Teen

Ever feel like you're trying to squeeze a 25-hour day into 24 hours? Yeah, it's a familiar vibe when your exams, projects, and social life all demand a piece of your time. Enter time-blocking, a method that can seriously upgrade your scheduling game. Think of it as Tetris, but instead of fitting blocks, you're scheduling chunks of your day to tackle different tasks effectively. This technique isn't just about cramming more into your day; it's about organizing your time in a way that maximizes productivity and minimizes stress.

Time-blocking is pretty straightforward: You divide your day into blocks of time, and each block is dedicated to accomplishing a specific task or group of tasks. This could mean setting aside specific hours for homework, gym time, or even scrolling through Instagram. The kicker? During each block, you focus solely on the set task, which reduces the scatterbrain feeling that comes from constant switching between tasks. It's about giving full attention to one segment of your to-do list at a time, which can boost your efficiency and help you churn through tasks quicker.

To get started, visualize your typical day and think about how you usually spend your hours. Now, shake that up by assigning specific tasks to specific times. For example, you might decide that 3 p.m. to 5 p.m. is for homework, 6 p.m. to 7 p.m. for dinner and chilling, and maybe 7 p.m. to 9 p.m. for more study or project work if needed. By mapping this out, you create a visual road map of your day, which can help you stay on track and keep procrastination at bay. Plus, it's satisfying to tick off tasks as you complete them during their dedicated time blocks.

 Exercise 13: The Time-Block Planner

At the start of each week, sit down with your planner or calendar and block out your time for the coming days. Start with your non-negotiables: school hours, extracurricular commitments, meals, and sleep. Then, look at your to-do list and assign each task to a specific time block. Be realistic about how long each task will take, and don't forget to schedule breaks.

As you go through your week, stick to your time blocks as much as possible. If a task takes less time than you allotted, use the extra minutes to get ahead on another task or take a short break. If you find yourself consistently underestimating or overestimating how long tasks take, adjust your future time blocks accordingly. At the end of the week, reflect on how well the time-blocking method worked for you. Did you feel more in control of your time and more productive overall? If so, make time-blocking a regular part of your planning process.

Prioritizing Your Digital Tasks: What Deserves Your Attention?

In a world where a single click can send you spiraling into hours of distraction, knowing how to prioritize your digital tasks is more crucial than ever. It's not just about managing time; it's about managing focus and intention. Let's crack the code on how to sift through the digital noise, spotlight what truly matters, and align your online activities with your real-world ambitions.

Think of your daily digital tasks like a bunch of open tabs in your browser. Some of these tabs are essential—they're your must-dos—while others are like those tabs you opened out of curiosity and forgot to close. Start by categorizing your digital tasks into "urgent," "important but not urgent," and "optional." Urgent tasks are those deadlines that can't be moved, like submitting an assignment by midnight. Important but not urgent tasks include things like scheduling a study session for next week. Optional tasks? That's checking the likes on your latest Insta post.

To effectively evaluate which tasks, fall into which category, ask yourself: Does this task align with my goals? What's the consequence of not doing it now? If it's aligned and postponing it could derail your plans, it's a high-priority task. If it's aligned but can be scheduled for later, slot it accordingly. And if it's not really adding value, consider dropping it or rescheduling it for your downtime. This method not only clears the clutter but also sharpens your focus, directing your energy to where it really counts.

Goal setting isn't just for New Year's resolutions—it's a vital tool for everyday productivity, especially in the digital realm. Start by defining what you want your digital engagement to achieve in the short and long term. Maybe it's improving your tech skills, expanding your knowledge on a subject through online courses, or building a network for career opportunities. Whatever it is, make your goals **SMART: specific, measurable, achievable, relevant, and time bound.**

Once your goals are set, align your digital tasks with these objectives. For instance, if your goal is to build a professional network, prioritize tasks like updating your LinkedIn profile or engaging with industry groups online. This alignment not only streamlines your digital activity but also ensures that every online interaction moves you a step closer to your goals. It's about making your digital life a ladder to your aspirations, not just a loop of distractions.

You can take charge of your digital productivity by categorizing tasks according to urgency and importance, aligning them with clear digital goals, and being intentional about how you engage with platforms like email and social media. It's about making conscious choices that steer your online activities toward what truly matters.

And if you ever feel overwhelmed by the digital flood, remember: You're the captain of this ship. You have the power to choose your direction and drop anchor when needed.

Case Study 10: The Priority-Driven Day

Ava was feeling overwhelmed by her digital to-do list. Between emails, social media notifications, online readings for class, and an ever-growing list of bookmarked articles she wanted to read, she didn't know where to start. She decided to try categorizing her tasks based on importance and urgency.

First, she identified the urgent and important tasks that needed to be done that day, like submitting a scholarship application and completing an online quiz. Next, she noted the important but not urgent tasks, like reading a chapter for next week's history class and researching summer internships. Finally, she put the non-essential tasks, like checking social media and reading articles for fun, in the optional category.

By tackling her to-do list in order of priority, Ava found she was able to focus on what really mattered and avoid getting sidetracked by less important tasks. She set specific times for checking social media and reading non-essential articles and stuck to them. At the end of the day, Ava felt a sense of accomplishment, knowing she had used her digital time intentionally and productively.

Mastering Your Digital Domain: The Power Is in Your Hands

It's easy to get swept up in the constant flow of digital distractions and demands, but remember—you are the master of your own attention. You have the power to choose what you focus on, when you focus on it, and for how long.

By using the strategies and techniques outlined in this chapter, you can start to reclaim control of your time and attention and channel them toward the things that truly matter to you.

Whether it's setting clear priorities, time-blocking your schedule, using productivity apps, or creating a focused study environment, find the methods that work best for you and make them a consistent part of your routine. It might take some trial and error, and that's okay. The key is to keep experimenting and refining your approach until you find your groove.

And don't forget the importance of balance. Yes, productivity is essential, but so is rest, play, and connecting with others. Make sure to schedule in time for the activities that recharge and inspire you, whether it's hanging out with friends, pursuing a hobby, or just taking a well-deserved nap.

As you navigate the challenges and opportunities of the digital world, remember that you are not alone. Reach out to your peers, teachers, and mentors for support and guidance. Share your strategies and struggles, and learn from each other. Together, we can help each other thrive in this ever-changing landscape.

So, go forth and conquer, my time-management warriors! Use the tools and techniques you've learned to make the most of every moment, both online and off. Chase your dreams, crush your goals, and don't let the distractions of the digital world hold you back. You've got this!

And if you ever feel like you're slipping back into old habits, just remember: Every day is a new opportunity to reset, refocus, and recommit to your priorities. Keep pushing forward, one focused time block at a time. The world is waiting for you to make your mark—go out there and seize the day!

Chapter 4

Financial Literacy for the Modern Teen

"Your wallet is more than a place for money—it's a tool for your dreams. Learn to manage it well, and watch your future unfold." - LLR Academy

It's time to talk about the green stuff—and no, I don't mean your science project on photosynthesis. I'm talking about cold, hard cash, or, more likely these days, the numbers on your banking app. In a world where money moves at the speed of a smartphone tap, having a solid grip on your finances is more important than ever.

But let's be real: Managing money as a teen can feel about as easy as navigating a TikTok dance challenge blindfolded. Between peer pressure to keep up with the latest trends, the temptation of in-app purchases, and the constant bombardment of financial advice from influencers, it's no wonder many teens feel lost in the money maze.

Fear not, my financially astute friends! This chapter is your trusty compass to guide you through the twists and turns of modern money management. We'll cover everything from budgeting basics to avoiding online scams, with plenty of real-world examples and practical tips along the way. By the end of this chapter, you'll be equipped with the knowledge and skills to take control of your financial future—no matter what the digital world throws your way.

So, grab your phone (or your piggy bank, if you're old-school like that), and let's dive in!

Budgeting Basics: Managing Your Money in a Digital World

Picture this: It's Friday night, and you're scrolling through your favorite food delivery app, drooling over the endless options. You've got a craving for sushi, but your wallet is giving you major side-eye. Suddenly, you remember that you already blew your budget on that trendy new gaming keyboard last week. Oops.

Sound familiar? In a world where money moves at the speed of a swipe, it's easy to lose track of where your cash is going.

That's where budgeting comes in—it's like a financial GPS that keeps you on track to reach your money goals.

At its core, budgeting is simple: It's about making sure you're not spending more than you're earning. But in practice, it can be a bit trickier, especially when you factor in the temptations of the digital world. Here are a few tips to help you create a budget that works for you:

- **Track your income and expenses:** Yes, it sounds about as thrilling as watching paint dry, but trust me—knowing where your money is coming from and where it's going is the foundation of any good budget. Use a budgeting app or good old-fashioned spreadsheet to keep tabs on your cash flow.

- **Categorize your spending:** Once you know where your money is going, it's time to put each expense into a category, like food, entertainment, or savings. This will help you see where you might be overspending and where you can cut back.

- **Set realistic goals:** Maybe you're saving up for a new laptop or you just want to have enough cash to hit the movies with your friends every weekend. Whatever your goals are, make sure they're specific, measurable, and achievable.

- **Be flexible:** Life happens, and sometimes unexpected expenses pop up (like when your little sister "accidentally" spills juice on your phone and you need a new one, stat). Don't beat yourself up if you have to adjust your budget from time to time—just get back on track as soon as you can.

- **Make it a habit:** Budgeting isn't a one-and-done deal—it's a lifelong skill that takes practice. Set aside a few minutes each week to review your budget and make any necessary adjustments. Over time, it'll become second nature, like scrolling through your Insta feed.

 ## Case Study 11: The Budgeting Boss

Meet Jordan, a 16-year-old self-proclaimed sneakerhead. He loved nothing more than adding the latest kicks to his collection—until he realized his shoe obsession was putting a serious dent in his wallet. Jordan knew he needed to get his spending under control, but he wasn't sure where to start.

That's when he discovered the power of budgeting. Using a budgeting app, Jordan started tracking his income (from his part-time job at the local grocery store) and his expenses (which, unsurprisingly, were mostly sneaker-related). He set a goal to save up for a special-edition pair of sneakers that were dropping in a few months and created a budget to help him get there.

Jordan allocated a certain amount of his paycheck to his sneaker fund each week, and he made sure to stick to his budget for other expenses like hanging out with friends and buying music. It wasn't always easy—there were plenty of temptations along the way—but by staying focused on his goal and adjusting his budget as needed, Jordan was able to save up enough cash to cop his dream sneakers. And the best part? He had developed a valuable life skill that would serve him well long after the sneakers had lost their new-shoe smell.

Budgeting might not be the most glamorous part of money management, but it's an essential tool for anyone who wants to take control of their financial future. By tracking your spending, setting goals, and staying flexible, you can create a budget that works for you—and maybe even have a little fun along the way. Who says spreadsheets can't be sexy?

Cryptocurrency and Teens: What You Need to Know

If you've been anywhere near the internet in the past few years, you've probably heard the buzz about cryptocurrency. From Bitcoin to Dogecoin, these digital assets have been making headlines and turning ordinary people into overnight millionaires (or so the stories go). But what exactly is cryptocurrency, and what do teens need to know about it?

First things first: Cryptocurrency is a type of digital or virtual currency that uses cryptography (a fancy word for coding) to secure and verify transactions. Unlike traditional currency, which is backed by governments and financial institutions, cryptocurrency operates on a decentralized network called the blockchain. This means that there's no central authority controlling the flow of funds—instead, transactions are recorded on a public ledger that anyone can access.

So, why are people so hyped about cryptocurrency? For one thing, it offers a level of anonymity and security that traditional financial systems can't match. Because transactions are recorded on the blockchain, they're virtually impossible to fake or tamper with. Plus, you don't need a bank account or credit card to use cryptocurrency—all you need is a digital wallet and an internet connection.

But before you start converting your allowance into Bitcoin, there are a few things you should keep in mind:

- **Cryptocurrency is highly volatile:** The value of cryptocurrencies can fluctuate wildly from day to day or even hour to hour. This means that while there's potential for big gains, there's also a risk of big losses.

- **Cryptocurrency is not regulated:** Unlike traditional financial institutions, there are no government regulations or protections in place for cryptocurrency. This means that if something goes wrong (like your digital wallet gets hacked), there's no guarantee you'll get your money back.

- **Cryptocurrency is not widely accepted:** While some businesses are starting to accept cryptocurrency as payment, it's still not as widely accepted as traditional currency. This means that if you want to use your cryptocurrency to buy something, you may need to convert it to cash first.

- **Cryptocurrency has a steep learning curve:** The world of cryptocurrency can be confusing and overwhelming, especially for beginners. Before you dive in, it's important to educate yourself on the basics of how cryptocurrency works and the potential risks and rewards.

Case Study 12: The Crypto Kid

Jose, a 17-year-old tech enthusiast, had been hearing about cryptocurrency for years. He was fascinated by the idea of a decentralized financial system and the potential for big returns on investment. So, when he received some money for his birthday, he decided to take the plunge and invest in Bitcoin.

At first, everything seemed to be going well. Jose watched with excitement as the value of his Bitcoin increased day by day. He started reading up on other cryptocurrencies and even convinced a few of his friends to invest as well. But then, the market took a turn. Overnight, the value of Bitcoin plummeted, and Jose watched helplessly as his investment shrank to a fraction of its original value.

Jose was devastated. He had put all his birthday money into Bitcoin, and now it was gone. He realized that he had gotten caught up in the hype without fully understanding the risks involved. He had fallen victim to the fear of missing out (FOMO) and had made an impulsive decision without doing his research.

Jose's story is a cautionary tale for any teen considering investing in cryptocurrency. While there's certainly potential for big gains, there's also a very real risk of losing everything. Before you invest any money in cryptocurrency, it's essential to educate yourself on the basics, understand the risks involved, and never invest more than you can afford to lose.

Cryptocurrency may be the wave of the future, but it's not a get-rich-quick scheme. Like any investment, it requires careful research, a long-term outlook, and a healthy dose of caution. So, before you jump on the crypto bandwagon, make sure you know what you're getting into—and always remember that there are no guarantees in the finance world.

Avoiding Online Scams: A Critical Thinking Guide

The internet can be a wild and wonderful place, full of endless opportunities for learning, entertainment, and connection. But it can also be a breeding ground for scams, frauds, and other nefarious activities designed to separate you from your hard-earned cash.

As a teen in the digital age, you're a prime target for online scammers. They know that you're tech-savvy and eager to make money, and they'll use every trick in the book to exploit those qualities. But fear not, my scam-savvy friends! With a little critical thinking and a healthy dose of skepticism, you can learn to spot the red flags and avoid falling victim to online scams.

Here are a few common types of online scams to watch out for:

- **Phishing scams:** These scams involve fake emails or websites that appear to be from legitimate companies or organizations, like your bank or social media platform. The goal is to trick you into revealing sensitive information, like your login credentials or credit card number.

- **Pyramid schemes:** Also known as multi-level marketing (MLM) schemes, these scams promise big returns for selling products or recruiting new members. In reality, most participants end up losing money while the people at the top of the pyramid rake in the profits.

- **Fake job offers:** Scammers will often post fake job listings or send unsolicited job offers via email or social media. These "jobs" may require you to pay upfront for training or supplies or involve illegal activities like money laundering.

- **Romance scams:** These scams involve fake online dating profiles designed to lure you into a relationship and eventually ask for money. The scammer may claim to need money for an emergency or to come visit you in person.

So, how can you avoid falling for these scams? Here are a few critical thinking tips:

- **Be skeptical of unsolicited offers:** If something sounds too good to be true (like a high-paying job with no experience required), it probably is.

- **Do your research:** Before you give any personal information or money to an online entity, do some digging to make sure they're legitimate. Look for reviews, contact information, and other signs of a real business or organization.

- **Don't respond to pressure tactics:** Scammers will often try to create a sense of urgency or scarcity to pressure you into making a decision quickly. If someone is pressuring you to act now or else miss out on a great opportunity, that's a red flag.

- **Trust your gut:** If something feels off or too good to be true, trust your instincts and walk away.

 ## Case Study 13: The Social Media Side Hustle

Maya, a 15-year-old aspiring influencer, was scrolling through her Instagram feed when she saw a post from a fellow influencer she admired. The post promised a "game-changing opportunity" to make money online by selling a new line of skincare products. All Maya had to do was pay a small fee to get started, and she could start earning commissions on sales right away.

Excited by the prospect of making money doing something she loved, Maya clicked on the link and started filling out the registration form. But as she was entering her credit card information, something stopped her. She realized that she didn't really know anything about this skincare company or the influencer promoting it. She decided to do some research before committing any money.

After a quick Google search, Maya discovered that the skincare company was actually a well-known MLM scheme that required participants to pay hefty fees upfront and recruit new members to make any real money. The influencer promoting it had likely been paid to do so and wasn't actually using or selling the products herself.

Maya breathed a sigh of relief, grateful she had trusted her gut and taken the time to do her research. She realized that not everything she saw on social media was as it seemed and that she needed to be more critical of the opportunities presented to her online.

Maya's experience is a common one for teens in the digital age. With so many scams and misleading offers out there, it's more important than ever to approach online opportunities with a critical eye. By being skeptical of unsolicited offers, doing your research, and trusting your instincts, you can avoid falling victim to online scams and protect your hard-earned money.

Remember, if something seems too good to be true, it probably is. Don't let the promise of easy money or a quick fix cloud your judgment. Take the time to think critically and do your due diligence, and you'll be well on your way to navigating the online world with confidence and savvy.

Financial Influencers: Separating Good Advice from the Gimmicks

In the age of social media, it seems like everyone, and their mother is a financial expert. From TikTok teens flaunting their stock market gains to Instagram influencers promoting the latest cryptocurrency craze, there's no shortage of people offering advice on how to make money online.

But how do you separate the legitimate financial gurus from the snake oil salesmen? How can you tell if a piece of financial advice is actually worth following or if it's just a gimmick designed to line someone else's pockets?

First things first: It's important to remember that just because someone has a large following or a flashy lifestyle doesn't mean they're an expert in finance. In fact, some of the most popular financial influencers out there are more interested in selling a lifestyle than providing sound financial advice.

So, how can you tell if a financial influencer is legit? Here are a few things to look for:

- **Transparency:** A reputable financial influencer will be transparent about their qualifications, their sources of income, and any potential conflicts of interest. They should also be willing to back up their claims with data and evidence.

- **Consistency:** If an influencer is constantly jumping from one hot investment trend to the next, that's a red flag. A good financial advisor will have a consistent, long-term approach to money management.

- **Realism:** Beware of influencers who promise overnight riches or guarantee returns on investment. In the world of finance, there are no sure things—only calculated risks and informed decisions.

- **Objectivity:** A trustworthy financial influencer will provide objective, unbiased advice tailored to your individual needs and goals. They shouldn't be pushing any particular product or service just because they're getting paid to do so.

Of course, even the most well-intentioned financial influencer can get it wrong sometimes. That's why it's essential to do your own research and think critically about any advice you receive. Here are a few tips for separating the good advice from the gimmicks:

- **Consider the source:** Is the person giving the advice a qualified financial professional or just someone with a large social media following? Do they have any credentials or experience in the field they're discussing?

- **Look for evidence:** Does the advice seem too good to be true? Is there any data or research to back up the claims being made? Be wary of influencers who rely on anecdotal evidence or personal testimonials to sell their ideas.

- **Consider the long-term:** Is the advice focused on short-term gains or long-term financial health? Be cautious of influencers who encourage risky or speculative investments without considering the potential downsides.

- **Trust your gut:** If something feels off or too good to be true, it probably is. Don't let the fear of missing out (FOMO) cloud your judgment or lead you to make impulsive decisions.

 Case Study 14: The Crypto Guru

Alyssa, a 16-year-old aspiring entrepreneur, had been following a popular financial influencer on TikTok for months. The influencer, who went by the name "CryptoKing," was always talking about the latest cryptocurrency trends and promising huge returns for those who invested early.

Alyssa was intrigued by the idea of making quick money and decided to take CryptoKing's advice. She used her savings to buy a few different cryptocurrencies he had recommended and waited eagerly for the profits to start rolling in.

As the weeks went by, Alyssa noticed that her investments weren't performing as well as CryptoKing had promised. In fact, some of the cryptocurrencies she had bought were starting to lose value. She started doing more research on CryptoKing and discovered that he had no real qualifications or experience in finance—he was simply a college student with a knack for social media marketing.

Alyssa realized that she had fallen for a gimmick and had put her hard-earned money at risk. She sold off her remaining cryptocurrency investments and vowed to be more critical of the financial advice she received online in the future.

Alyssa's experience is a cautionary tale for any teen who's thinking about taking financial advice from social media influencers. While there are certainly some legitimate experts out there, it's important to approach any advice with a healthy dose of skepticism and do your own research before making any investment decisions.

Remember, just because someone has a large following or a flashy lifestyle doesn't mean they have your best interests at heart. Some influencers are more interested in promoting their brand or selling a particular product than providing sound financial advice.

So, how can you tell if a financial influencer is worth following? Look for someone who is transparent about their qualifications and experience, provides evidence to back up their claims, and offers realistic, objective advice tailored to your individual needs and goals.

Most importantly, trust your judgment. If something seems too good to be true or doesn't align with your personal values and risk tolerance, don't be afraid to walk away. There's no shame in taking a cautious approach to your finances, especially when you're just starting out.

At the end of the day, the most valuable investment you can make is in yourself. By taking the time to educate yourself about personal finance, setting clear goals and boundaries, and seeking out reliable sources of information and advice, you'll be well on your way to building a strong financial foundation that will serve you well throughout your life.

Planning for the Future: Savings Strategies for Teens

Okay, I know what you're thinking. *Savings? But I'm young and fabulous! I've got plenty of time to worry about that boring stuff later.* And hey, I get it. When you're a teen, it's easy to get caught up in the moment and forget about the future.

But here's the thing: The earlier you start saving, the more time your money has to grow. And I'm not just talking about saving for a rainy day (although that's important, too). I'm talking about saving for the big stuff—college, a car, your first apartment, maybe even retirement (I know, I know, that's like a million years away).

So, how can you start building your savings as a teen? Here are a few strategies to get you started:

- **Set a savings goal:** Whether it's a new phone, a summer road trip, or your first semester of college tuition, having a specific goal in mind can help you stay motivated and on track.

- **Make a budget:** Remember that budgeting stuff we talked about earlier? Yeah, it's important for saving, too. By keeping track of your income and expenses, you can figure out how much you can realistically set aside each month.

- **Pay yourself first:** As soon as you get your paycheck or allowance, put a portion of it straight into your savings account. That way, you're not tempted to spend it on something else.

- **Look for ways to earn extra money:** Whether it's babysitting, tutoring, or starting a side hustle, finding ways to boost your income can help you reach your savings goals faster.

- **Take advantage of compound interest:** Okay, bear with me here—this is where things get a little math-y. Compound interest is basically the interest you earn on your interest. So, the earlier you start saving, the more time your money has to compound and grow.

But saving money isn't only about the numbers. It's also about developing good financial habits that will serve you well throughout your life. Here are a few more tips for building a strong savings mindset:

- **Practice delayed gratification:** Instead of buying something right away, try waiting a few days or even a few weeks. You might find that the urge to spend passes, and you can put that money toward your savings instead.

- **Avoid lifestyle inflation:** As you start to earn more money, it can be tempting to upgrade your lifestyle accordingly. Try to resist the urge to spend more just because you can. Instead, use that extra income to boost your savings.

- **Educate yourself:** The more you know about personal finance, the better equipped you'll be to make smart money decisions. Read books, listen to podcasts, and seek out reliable sources of financial advice.

- **Celebrate your progress:** Saving money can be a long and sometimes challenging process. Take time to acknowledge and celebrate your successes along the way, no matter how small they may seem.

Case Study 15: The Savings Superhero

Reid, a 17-year-old high school senior, had always been pretty good with money. He had a part-time job at a local restaurant and tried to save a little bit of each paycheck. But with college looming on the horizon, he knew he needed to step up his savings game.

Reid sat down and made a list of his expenses and income. He realized he was spending a lot of money on eating out and buying new video games every month. He decided to cut back on those expenses and put the extra money toward his college savings instead.

He also started looking for ways to earn extra money. He started tutoring younger students in math and science and even started a small lawn care business on the weekends. Every extra dollar he earned went straight into his savings account.

Over time, Reid watched his savings grow. He was amazed at how quickly the money added up, thanks to the power of compound interest. By the time he graduated from high school, he had saved enough to cover his first year of college tuition and then some.

But Reid's savings journey didn't stop there. He continued to practice good financial habits throughout college and beyond.

He avoided taking on too much student debt, lived below his means, and always made saving a priority. By the time he landed his first "real" job after graduation, he had a solid financial foundation that set him up for long-term success.

Reid's story is proof that it's never too early to start saving for the future. By setting clear goals, making a budget, and looking for ways to earn extra income, you can start building your savings muscle today.

And remember, saving money isn't about depriving yourself of the things you love. It's about making smart choices and prioritizing your long-term financial health. So, go ahead and treat yourself every once in a while—just make sure you're putting some of that money away for the future, too.

Who knows? Maybe one day you'll look back on your teenage self and thank them for being such a savings superhero. Your future self will definitely appreciate it.

The True Cost of In-App Purchases and How to Resist Them

Picture this: You're playing your favorite mobile game, crushing candy or battling monsters or whatever it is you do. You're on a roll, racking up points and leveling up like a boss. But then, suddenly, you hit a wall. You're out of lives, or you need a special item to progress, or you just really want that shiny new character skin.

And then, like a beacon of hope in a sea of frustration, you see it: The option to make an in-app purchase. Just a few taps and a couple of bucks and you can be back in the game, stronger than ever. It's so tempting, so easy, so... harmless, right?

Wrong. In-app purchases might seem like a quick fix, but they can add up quickly and do some serious damage to your wallet.

And the worst part? They're designed to be addictive, to keep you coming back for more and more.

But fear not, my savvy gamers! There are ways to resist the siren song of in-app purchases and keep your hard-earned cash where it belongs (i.e., not in the pockets of greedy game developers). Here are a few tips:

- **Know the true cost:** That $0.99 power-up might not seem like much, but if you're buying them regularly, it can add up fast. Do the math and figure out how much you're really spending on in-app purchases each month.

- **Set a budget:** If you do decide to make in-app purchases, set a strict budget for yourself and stick to it. Don't let yourself get carried away in the heat of the moment.

- **Look for free alternatives:** Many games offer free ways to earn the same items or power-ups that you can buy with real money. They might take a little more time and effort, but they'll save you cash in the long run.

- **Resist the pressure:** Game developers use all sorts of psychological tricks to get you to make in-app purchases, like time-sensitive offers or social pressure from other players. Don't fall for it! Remember, it's just a game—there's no real-world consequence for not having the latest and greatest gear.

- **Know when to walk away:** If you find yourself getting too caught up in the cycle of in-app purchases, it might be time to take a break from the game altogether. There's no shame in admitting that something isn't good for you and making a change.

But in-app purchases aren't just a problem for gamers. They can show up in all sorts of apps, from fitness trackers to photo filters. And the same principles apply: Know the true cost, set a budget, look for free alternatives, resist the pressure, and know when to walk away.

Case Study 16: The In-App Purchase Addict

Faris, a 14-year-old gaming enthusiast, had always been careful with his money. He saved up his allowance and birthday cash and rarely bought anything without carefully considering the cost. But when he discovered the world of mobile gaming, everything changed.

At first, Faris stuck to free games and avoided in-app purchases altogether. But as he got more invested in his favorite games, he started to feel the pressure to keep up with his friends and guildmates.

He started making small purchases here and there just to stay competitive.

Before he knew it, Faris was spending hundreds of dollars a month on in-app purchases. He was buying new characters, power-ups, and virtual currency like it was going out of style. His savings dwindled, and he started begging his parents for more money to feed his habit.

Finally, Faris's parents sat him down for a serious talk. They helped him see how much money he was really spending on games and how it was affecting his financial health. Faris was shocked—he had no idea he had spent so much.

Together, they came up with a plan to help Faris break his in-app purchase addiction. They set a strict budget for gaming expenses, and Faris agreed to stick to it. He also started looking for free alternatives to the items he wanted to buy, like earning rewards through gameplay instead of purchasing them.

It wasn't easy, but over time, Faris was able to wean himself off of in-app purchases and get his spending under control. He still enjoyed gaming, but he did it in a way that was healthy and sustainable for his wallet.

Faris's story is a cautionary tale for anyone who's ever been tempted by the allure of in-app purchases. It's easy to get carried away and spend more than you intended, especially when you're caught up in the heat of the moment.

By being mindful of your spending, setting clear boundaries, and finding free alternatives, when possible, you can enjoy your favorite apps and games without breaking the bank. And who knows? Maybe you'll even find that the sense of accomplishment that comes from earning rewards through gameplay is more satisfying than any in-app purchase could ever be.

So, go forth and game on, my friends. Just remember to keep one eye on your wallet and one finger on the "cancel" button. Your future self (and your bank account) will thank you.

Chapter 5

Physical and Mental Well-being in a Digital Age

"Balance your screen time with green time; your mind and body thrive when they're in harmony." – LLR Academy

The digital world can be a double-edged sword when it comes to our health. On one hand, we have access to endless resources and tools that can help us stay fit, eat right, and manage stress. On the other hand, we're constantly bombarded with screens, notifications, and online pressures that can take a toll on our sleep, self-esteem, and overall sense of balance.

But fear not! With a little mindfulness and strategic tech use, we can learn to thrive in the digital landscape while still prioritizing our physical and mental well-being. In this chapter, we'll explore practical tips and strategies for:

- finding your perfect screen time balance
- leveraging technology for fitness
- combating digital stress and anxiety
- eating healthy in a fast-food era
- navigating the complex relationship between social media and self-esteem
- knowing when it's time to take a digital detox

So, put on your favorite athleisure, grab a healthy snack, and let's dive in! Your mind and body will thank you.

Screen Time and Sleep: Finding Your Perfect Balance

It's late at night, and you're lying in bed, scrolling through your social media feeds. You tell yourself, "Just five more minutes," but before you know it, an hour has passed, and you're still wide awake—your brain buzzing with the glow of your screen. Sound familiar?

In today's 24/7 digital world, it's all too easy to let screen time interfere with our sleep. But here's the thing: Sleep is non-negotiable when it comes to our physical and mental health.

It's essential for everything from cognitive function to emotional regulation to immune system support.

So, how can we find that perfect balance between staying connected and getting enough rest? Here are a few tips:

- **Set a digital curfew:** Establish a specific time each night when you'll put away your screens and start winding down for bed. Stick to it as consistently as possible, even on weekends.

- **Create a screen-free sleep environment:** Keep your bedroom a sacred space for rest, free from the distractions of TVs, laptops, and phones. If you need your phone for an alarm, try putting it on airplane mode or using a separate alarm clock.

- **Use blue light blocking tools:** The blue light emitted by our screens can interfere with our natural sleep-wake cycle. Try using blue light blocking glasses or installing a blue light filter app on your devices to minimize the impact.

- **Find screen-free ways to relax before bed:** Instead of scrolling through your phone, try reading a book, taking a warm bath, or practicing some gentle stretching or meditation to help you unwind.

- **Be mindful of your daytime screen habits, too:** The more time we spend on screens during the day, the harder it can be to disconnect at night. Try taking regular screen breaks, getting outside for some natural light, and engaging in non-digital hobbies and activities.

Case Study 17: The Social Media Slumber Struggle

Kira, a 16-year-old high school student, had always been a night owl. She loved staying up late, chatting with friends, and scrolling through her social media feeds. But as her schoolwork and extracurricular activities ramped up, she found herself struggling to stay awake and focused during the day.

Kira knew she needed to make a change, but the thought of giving up her late-night social media time felt impossible. It was her way of unwinding and staying connected with her friends.

With the help of her parents and a school counselor, Kira came up with a plan to gradually shift her screen habits and prioritize her sleep. She started by setting a digital curfew of 10 p.m., an hour before her usual bedtime. At first, putting her phone away so early felt strange and even a little lonely, but she found that reading a book or journaling before bed actually helped her feel more relaxed and ready for sleep.

Kira also made a point of taking regular screen breaks during the day, stepping away from her laptop and phone to stretch, go for a quick walk, or chat with a friend in person. She found that these small breaks helped her feel more focused and less overwhelmed by her digital life.

Over time, Kira started to notice a difference in her energy levels and overall well-being. She was sleeping better, feeling more alert during the day, and even enjoying her social media time more when she did allow herself to indulge.

Kira's story is a reminder that finding balance in our digital lives is an ongoing process, one that requires intentionality, self-awareness, and a willingness to make changes when necessary. By prioritizing our sleep and being mindful of our screen habits, we can create a healthier, more sustainable relationship with technology

Digital Fitness: Leveraging Technology for Physical Health

When it comes to staying fit and active in the digital age, technology can be our best friend or our worst enemy. On the one hand, we have access to endless fitness apps, online workouts, and high-tech gadgets that can help us track our progress and stay motivated.

On the other hand, we're often glued to our screens, sitting for hours on end and neglecting our physical health.

But what if we could harness the power of technology to support our fitness goals rather than hinder them? Here are a few ways to leverage digital tools for physical health:

- **Use fitness tracking apps and wearables:** From simple step counters to high-tech smartwatches, there are countless tools available to help you track your activity levels, monitor your heart rate, and set fitness goals. Find one that works for you and use it to stay accountable and motivated.

- **Try online workouts and fitness classes:** Can't make it to the gym? No problem! There are tons of online resources for workouts and fitness classes, from yoga and Pilates to HIIT and strength training. Many of these resources are free or low-cost, and you can do them from the comfort of your own home.

- **Join online fitness communities and challenges:** Sometimes, a little social support and friendly competition can be just the motivation you need to stay on track with your fitness goals. Look for online communities or challenges related to your favorite type of exercise, whether it's running, cycling, or dancing.

- **Gamify your workouts with virtual reality and other immersive technologies:** From VR fitness games to interactive home gym equipment, there are plenty of high-tech ways to make exercise feel more like play. While these tools can be pricey, they can also be a fun and engaging way to mix up your routine.

- **Balance screen time with real-world activity:** As much as technology can support your fitness goals, it's important to remember that nothing beats the benefits of real-world movement and activity. Make a point of stepping away from your screens regularly to stretch, go for a walk, or engage in your favorite physical hobbies and sports.

 Exercise 14: The Digital Fitness Challenge

Ready to put these digital fitness strategies into action? Here's a simple challenge to get you started:

- **Set a specific fitness goal** for the next month, whether it's hitting a certain number of steps per day, trying a new type of online workout, or training for a virtual 5K race.

- **Choose one or two digital tools**, such as a fitness app or online community, to help you track your progress and stay motivated.

- **Make a plan for incorporating** regular screen-free movement and activity into your daily routine, such as taking a morning walk or trying a new outdoor hobby.

- **At the end of the month**, reflect on your progress and how your digital fitness tools supported (or hindered) your goals. What worked well? What could you improve or adjust going forward?

- **Share your experience** with a friend or family member or post about it on social media to inspire others to join the digital fitness revolution!

Remember, the key to digital fitness is finding a balance that works for you. Don't be afraid to experiment with different tools and strategies until you find a combination that feels sustainable and enjoyable. Above all, remember to listen to your body and prioritize your physical health, both on and off the screen.

Mindfulness in Motion: Combating Digital Stress and Anxiety

Let's face it: The digital world can be a stressful place. From the constant pings of notifications to the pressure to always be "on" and available, it's easy to feel overwhelmed and anxious in the face of technology. But what if we could use that same technology to cultivate a sense of mindfulness and calm?

Enter the world of digital mindfulness—the practice of using technology to support our mental health and well-being. From meditation apps to virtual reality relaxation experiences, there are countless tools available to help us slow down, breathe, and find a sense of inner peace amidst the digital noise.

Here are a few ways to incorporate mindfulness into your digital life:

- **Try a meditation or mindfulness app:** Apps like Headspace, Calm, and Insight Timer offer guided meditations, breathing exercises, and other mindfulness practices that you can access anytime, anywhere. Start with just a few minutes a day and build up from there.

- **Take regular screen-free breaks:** Set aside dedicated times each day to step away from your devices and engage in mindful, screen-free activities like deep breathing, stretching, or simply sitting in silence. Even just a few minutes can help you reset and recharge.

- **Practice digital gratitude:** Instead of getting caught up in the negative aspects of technology, try focusing on the ways it enriches your life. Keep a digital gratitude journal where you jot down a few things you're thankful for each day or share your appreciation with friends and followers online.

- **Use technology to connect with nature:** From virtual hikes and beach walks to live webcams of natural wonders around the world, there are plenty of ways to use technology to tap into the calming power of nature. Make a point of incorporating these virtual nature breaks into your daily routine.

- **Create a mindful digital environment:** Just like you can create a peaceful physical environment with things like plants, calming colors, and cozy textures, you can also curate a mindful digital space. Choose backgrounds and screensavers that inspire a sense of calm, organize your files and apps in a way that feels intuitive and uncluttered, and be intentional about the online content you consume

 ### Case Study 18: The Digital Meditation Miracle

Hazel, a 17-year-old student, had always been an anxious person. But when the COVID-19 pandemic hit, and her entire life moved online—from school to socializing to extracurricular activities—her anxiety skyrocketed. She found herself constantly refreshing her news feeds, worrying about the future, and feeling increasingly disconnected from her friends and hobbies.

At the suggestion of her school counselor, Hazel decided to give digital mindfulness a try. She started by downloading a popular meditation app and committing to just five minutes of guided practice each morning before starting her online classes.

At first, Hazel found it hard to quiet her racing thoughts and focus on her breath. However, as she continued to practice each day, she started to notice small shifts in her mindset and mood. She felt a little more grounded, a little more present, and a little more able to handle the stresses of her digital life.

Inspired by her progress, Hazel started incorporating other mindful tech habits into her routine, like taking regular screen-free breaks to stretch or go for a quick walk around the block. She also made a point of seeking out positive, uplifting content online, from inspiring Instagram accounts to funny animal videos that never failed to make her smile.

Over time, Hazel found that her digital mindfulness practice had become an essential part of her self-care routine—a way to find moments of calm and clarity amidst the chaos of the online world.

And while her anxiety hadn't disappeared completely, she felt better equipped to manage it, one mindful breath at a time.

Hazel's story is a powerful reminder that technology doesn't have to be the enemy of our mental health. In fact, it can be a valuable tool for cultivating mindfulness and resilience in the face of digital stress and anxiety. By being intentional about how we use technology and incorporating mindful practices into our daily routines, we can create a more balanced, peaceful relationship with the digital world

Nutrition Tracking and Digital Tools: Eating Healthy in a Fast-Food Era

In a world of drive-thrus, food delivery apps, and vending machines on every corner, eating healthy can feel harder than solving a Rubik's cube blindfolded. But just like we can use technology to support our physical fitness and mental well-being, we can also harness the power of digital tools to help us make better nutrition choices.

From meal planning apps and grocery delivery services to nutrition tracking software and online cooking classes, there's a whole buffet of digital resources available to help us eat smart in a fast-food era. Here are a few tips for leveraging these tools:

- **Use a nutrition-tracking app to monitor your macros and micronutrients:** Apps like MyFitnessPal, Lose It! and Cronometer allow you to log your meals and snacks, set nutrition goals, and get insights into your eating habits over time. While it's important not to get too obsessive about tracking, these tools can be a helpful way to build awareness and make more informed food choices.

- **Try grocery delivery or meal kit services for healthier home cooking:** Services like HelloFresh, Blue Apron, and Instacart make it easier than ever to get fresh, nutritious ingredients delivered right to your doorstep. With pre-portioned ingredients and step-by-step recipes, these services take the guesswork out of healthy cooking and can help you save time and reduce food waste.

- **Seek out online nutrition education and recipe resources:** From nutrition blogs and podcasts to YouTube cooking tutorials and virtual cooking classes, there's a wealth of free and low-cost resources available to help you learn about healthy eating and expand your culinary skills. Make a point of seeking out reputable, science-based sources and experimenting with new recipes and ingredients.

- **Use technology to practice mindful eating:** Just like you can use apps to support mindfulness in other areas of our lives, you can also use them to cultivate a more mindful relationship with food. Try using a mindful eating app like Am I Hungry? or Eat Right Now to practice slowing down, savoring your food, and tuning into your body's hunger and fullness cues.

- **Remember that technology is just one tool in your healthy eating tool kit:** While digital resources can be incredibly helpful, they're not a substitute for listening to your body, enjoying whole foods, and finding a balanced approach to nutrition that works for you. Use technology as a support system, but don't let it become a source of stress or obsession.

 Exercise 15: The Healthy Eating Experiment

Ready to put these digital nutrition tools to the test? Here's a fun experiment to try:

1. **Set a specific nutrition goal** for the next week, whether it's eating more vegetables, reducing your sugar intake, or trying a new healthy recipe each day.

2. **Choose one or two digital tools** to help you work toward this goal, such as a nutrition tracking app, grocery delivery service, or

online cooking class.

3. **Keep a journal throughout** the week to reflect on your experience. What did you learn about your eating habits? How did the digital tools support (or hinder) your goal? What challenges or successes did you encounter along the way?

4. **At the end of the week, assess your progress** and consider how you might incorporate these digital nutrition strategies into your longer-term healthy eating plan. What worked well? What could you improve or adjust going forward?

5. **Share your experience** with a friend or family member, or post about it on social media to inspire others to join you in eating healthy in the digital age!

Remember, healthy eating is a lifelong journey, not a destination. By experimenting with different tools and strategies, staying curious and open-minded, and being patient with yourself along the way, you can build a positive, sustainable relationship with food that supports your physical and mental well-being—one bite at a time

The Relationship Between Social Media and Self-Esteem

If you've ever found yourself scrolling through Instagram and feeling like everyone else's life is more glamorous, exciting, or picture-perfect than your own, you're not alone. In fact, research has shown that social media use can have a significant impact on self-esteem and body image, especially for teens and young adults (Goldfield, 2023).

But why is this the case? And what can we do to cultivate a healthier, more positive relationship with social media and our self-worth? Let's dive in.

One of the main reasons that social media can be so damaging to our self-esteem is that it often presents a curated, filtered version of reality. When we're constantly bombarded with images of perfect bodies, lavish lifestyles, and flawless selfies, it's easy to feel like we don't measure up. We start to compare ourselves to an unrealistic standard and feel inadequate or dissatisfied with our own lives.

Another factor is the pressure to constantly perform and seek validation online. When we tie our self-worth to the number of likes, comments, or followers we receive, we're setting ourselves up for a roller coaster of emotions. We might feel great when a post goes viral but devastated when it flops—and this constant seeking of external validation can take a toll on our mental health.

So, what can we do to break free from this cycle and build a healthier sense of self-esteem in the digital age? Here are a few strategies to try:

- **Curate your feed with intention:** Follow accounts that inspire and uplift you rather than ones that make you feel bad about yourself. Don't be afraid to unfollow or mute accounts that trigger negative self-talk or comparison.

- **Practice digital gratitude:** Instead of focusing on what you lack, make a habit of regularly posting about the things you're grateful for in your own life. This could be anything from a beautiful sunset to a supportive friend to a personal accomplishment you're proud of.

- **Limit your screen time:** Set boundaries around when and how often you check social media and make a point of engaging in screen-free activities that bring you joy and fulfillment. The less time you spend scrolling, the less power those filtered images will have over your self-esteem.

- **Engage in real-world self-care:** Make a point of doing things that make you feel good in your offline life, whether it's taking a bubble bath, going for a nature walk, or practicing a favorite hobby. The more you prioritize your well-being, the less you'll rely on social media for validation.

- **Remember that social media is just one part of your story:** Your worth as a person is not defined by your online presence or popularity. Focus on cultivating a strong sense of self that is rooted in your values, passions, and real-life relationships—not just your digital ones.

 ## Case Study 19: The Self-Esteem Social Media Makeover

Alex, a 15-year-old high school student, had always been confident and outgoing. However, when they started spending more time on social media, they noticed a shift in their self-esteem. Alex found themselves constantly comparing their life to the highlight reels of their classmates and feeling like they didn't measure up.

One day, after a particularly tough bout of social media scrolling, Alex decided enough was enough. They realized that their online habits were taking a toll on their mental health and self-worth, and they wanted to make a change.

Alex started by unfollowing accounts that made them feel bad about themselves and seeking out content that was more positive and uplifting. They made a point of posting about the things they were grateful for in their own life rather than trying to compete with others' curated images.

Alex also set clear boundaries around their social media use, limiting themselves to just 30 minutes per day and making a point of engaging in screen-free activities that brought them joy, like playing music and spending time with friends in person.

Over time, Alex started to notice a shift in their mindset. They felt more grounded and self-assured, less caught up in the comparison game of social media. They still enjoyed connecting with friends online but no longer tied their self-worth to their digital popularity.

Alex's story reminds us that while social media can be a fun and enriching part of our lives, we should use it in a way that supports, rather than undermines, our self-esteem. By being intentional about the content we consume and the boundaries we set, we can cultivate a healthier relationship with both social media and ourselves

Detoxing Digitally: Taking Time Off for Your Mental Health

As much as we love the digital world and all its shiny distractions, sometimes we need to take a step back and unplug for the sake of our mental health.

Digital detoxes, or intentional breaks from technology, have become increasingly popular in recent years as a way to combat the stress, anxiety, and burnout that can come from constant connectivity. Whether it's a day, a week, or even just a few hours, taking time away from screens can help us recharge, refocus, and reconnect with ourselves and the world around us.

So, how can you incorporate digital detoxes into your own life? Here are a few tips:

- **Start small:** If the idea of going a whole day without your phone feels overwhelming, start with just a few hours at a time. Put your devices away during meals, before bed, or while spending time with friends and family. Gradually build up to longer stretches as you get more comfortable.

- **Make it a regular practice:** Rather than waiting until you're on the brink of burnout, make digital detoxes a regular part of your self-care routine. This could mean designating one day a week as a screen-free day or taking a mini detox each evening before bed.

- **Find screen-free activities that bring you joy:** To make your digital detoxes more enjoyable and rewarding, have a list of offline activities you love to turn to. This could be anything from reading a book to trying a new hobby to exploring your local community.

- **Communicate your boundaries:** Let your friends and family, and coworkers know when you'll be unplugging so they know not to expect an immediate response. You might even inspire them to join you in your digital detox practice!

- **Be kind to yourself:** If you slip up or find yourself reaching for your phone out of habit, don't beat yourself up. Digital detoxing is a practice, not a perfection. Celebrate your progress and keep coming back to your intention to unplug.

 Case Study 20: The Digital Detox Diaries

Maya, a 20-year-old college student, was always the first to admit she was addicted to her phone. From the moment she woke up to the moment she went to bed, Maya was glued to her screens—scrolling through social media, texting friends, and binge-watching Netflix. But as her screen time started to take a toll on her sleep, concentration, and overall well-being, Maya knew something had to change.

Inspired by a friend who had recently completed a week-long digital detox, Maya decided to give it a try. She started by setting some clear boundaries: no phone use during meals, no screens for an hour before bed, and one full day each week completely unplugged.

At first, the detox was harder than Maya had anticipated. She found herself reaching for her phone out of habit and feeling anxious without the constant stimulation of notifications and alerts. But as she leaned into screen-free activities like reading, hiking, and catching up with friends in person, Maya started to feel a shift.

She slept better, felt more focused and creative, and noticed a newfound sense of presence and connection in her daily life. While Maya knew that completely swearing off technology wasn't realistic or desirable for her lifestyle, she realized that regular digital detoxes were an essential part of her self-care tool kit. By being more intentional about her screen time and prioritizing offline activities, Maya found a healthier balance that supported her mental health and well-being.

Maya's story is a powerful reminder that in a world of constant connectivity, sometimes the greatest act of self-love is simply taking a step back and unplugging. Whether it's for an hour, a day, or a week, giving ourselves permission to disconnect from the digital noise and reconnect with ourselves and the world around us can be a game-changer for our mental health and overall happiness.

We've covered a lot of ground in this chapter, At the end of the day, the key to thriving in the digital world is finding what works for you. There's no one-size-fits-all approach to digital wellness—it's all about experimenting, adapting, and being kind to yourself along the way.

I hope this chapter has left you feeling empowered and inspired to take charge of your digital well-being. Whether you're a teen navigating the ups and downs of social media, a young adult striving for work-life balance in a hyperconnected world, or simply a human being trying to find your way in the digital age, know that you have the power to create a relationship with technology that supports your health, happiness, and highest self.

So, go forth and thrive, my digital wellness warriors! The world (both online and off) needs your unique light and energy. Just remember to unplug every once in a while, and savor the magic of the present moment. Because, in the end, that's what life is all about.

Happy (digital) well-being, everyone!

Chapter 6

The Ethics of Digital Life

"In the digital world, let your integrity be your guide. Stand firm in your values, even when no one's watching." – LLR Academy

In the vast, ever-evolving landscape of the digital world, it's easy to feel like a small fish in a big pond. But here's the thing: Every action we take online, no matter how small, has ripple effects that can shape the digital ecosystem for better or worse.

From how we handle our personal data to how we treat others in virtual spaces, our digital choices have real-world consequences. As technology becomes increasingly intertwined with every aspect of our lives, it's more important than ever to approach our online behavior with intention, compassion, and a strong ethical compass.

In this chapter, we'll examine some of the most pressing ethical challenges of the digital age, including:

- managing your digital footprint with privacy and security in mind
- understanding and standing against cyberbullying
- sharing responsibly and ethically in the age of viral content
- navigating the legalities of consent and content online
- using your digital voice for activism and positive change
- treating others with respect and kindness in virtual spaces

Together, we can create a more mindful, responsible, and compassionate online culture—one click at a time.

Your Digital Footprint: Privacy, Security, and Ethics

Imagine this: Every time you step outside your house, you leave a trail of footprints behind you. Now, imagine that those footprints contain intimate details about your life—your habits, your relationships, your deepest secrets. Imagine that anyone in the world could follow those footprints and piece together a detailed picture of who you are.

Welcome to the world of your digital footprint.

Every time we use the internet, we leave behind a trail of data—from the websites we visit and the searches we conduct to the posts we like and the messages we send. This data can be incredibly valuable, not just to companies looking to target us with ads but also to hackers, scammers, and other bad actors who might use it to exploit us.

So, how can we navigate this digital landscape with our privacy, security, and ethics intact? Here are a few key strategies:

- **Be mindful of what you share:** Before you post something online, ask yourself: Is this information I want to be public and permanent? If not, think twice before hitting "share."

- **Use privacy settings:** Most social media platforms and online services offer privacy settings that allow you to control who can see your posts and profile information. Take the time to review and adjust these settings regularly.

- **Practice good password hygiene:** Use strong, unique passwords for each of your online accounts, and consider using a password manager to keep track of them all. Enable two-factor authentication whenever possible for an extra layer of security.

- **Be wary of phishing and scams:** If an email, message, or website seems suspicious or too good to be true, trust your instincts. Don't click on links or download attachments from unknown sources.

- **Consider the ethical implications of your data:** Before using a new app or service, read the privacy policy and terms of service carefully. How will your data be used and shared? Do the company's values align with your own?

 ## Case Study 21: The Social Media Snafu

Jade, a 22-year-old recent college grad, was excited to start her first "real" job at a promising tech startup. She had worked hard to clean up her social media presence during her job search, making sure to delete any old posts or photos that might raise eyebrows with potential employers.

But a few weeks into her new gig, Jade was called into her boss's office for a serious chat. Someone had anonymously sent the company screenshots of some offensive jokes and racy photos that Jade had shared on Twitter back in high school—posts she thought she had deleted long ago.

Jade was mortified and terrified that she might lose her job over her teenage social media antics. Luckily, her boss was understanding and gave her a second chance, but the experience taught Jade a valuable lesson about the permanence of her digital footprint.

From that day forward, Jade made a point of being extra cautious about what she posted online. She regularly googled herself to keep tabs on her digital reputation, and she made a habit of asking herself, "Would I want my boss or grandma to see this?" before sharing anything. She also started using more secure privacy settings and being more selective about which apps and services she used.

Jade's story is a powerful reminder that in the digital age, our past can come back to haunt us in unexpected ways. But by being proactive about managing our digital footprint, we can take control of our online reputation and avoid potential pitfalls down the road.

Cyberbullying: Understanding It and Standing Against It

It's a sad but undeniable fact of the digital age: Cyberbullying is a major problem, especially for teens and young adults. A 2019 survey found that nearly 37% of young people between the ages of 12 and 17 had been bullied online in the past year—a number that has likely only grown in the age of remote learning and increased screen time.

But what exactly is cyberbullying, and how can we stand against it? Put simply, cyberbullying is the use of digital technologies—such as social media, messaging apps, or online forums—to harass, threaten, embarrass, or target another person. It can take many forms, from spreading rumors and sharing embarrassing photos to sending threatening messages and encouraging others to gang up on a target.

The effects of cyberbullying can be devastating, leading to anxiety, depression, and even suicidal thoughts and behaviors in some cases. And because it can happen anytime, anywhere, and often anonymously, it can feel like there's no escape for those who are being targeted.

So, what can we do to prevent and combat cyberbullying? Here are a few key strategies:

- **Speak up:** Don't be a passive bystander if you see someone being bullied online. Report the behavior to the platform or a trusted adult, and reach out to the person being targeted to offer support.

- **Set clear boundaries:** Make it clear to your friends and followers that you won't tolerate bullying or harassment on your profiles or channels. If someone crosses a line, don't hesitate to block or report them.

- **Practice digital empathy:** Before you post something online, ask yourself: Could this be hurtful or embarrassing to someone else? Put yourself in others' shoes and aim to spread kindness, not cruelty.

- **Know your resources:** If you or someone you know is being cyberbullied, there are resources available to help. Check out websites like StopBullying.gov and the Cyberbullying Research Center for tips, hotlines, and reporting tools.

- **Be an upstander, not a bystander:** Stand up for what's right, even when it's not easy. Be a role model for compassion and courage in the face of cruelty.

Case Study 22: The Anti-Bullying Activist

Tyler, a 16-year-old high school student, had always been a bit of a loner. He was shy, quirky, and often felt like he didn't quite fit in with his classmates. But when he started getting harassed and bullied online by some of the popular kids at school, his isolation took a dark turn.

At first, Tyler tried to ignore the cruel comments and mocking memes that filled his social media feeds. But as the bullying escalated and started spilling over into his real life, he felt increasingly hopeless and alone. He stopped wanting to go to school, and his grades started to slip.

One day, after a particularly vicious round of online taunts, Tyler decided enough was enough. He reached out to a teacher he trusted and told her what had been going on. The teacher connected him with the school counselor, who helped him come up with a plan to address the bullying and take care of his mental health.

Inspired by his own experience, Tyler started an anti-bullying club at his school, where students could come together to support each other and raise awareness about the impact of cyberbullying. He organized events, led workshops, and even spoke at school assemblies about the importance of digital empathy and allyship.

Over time, Tyler started to see a shift in his school's culture. More and more students were speaking out against bullying and standing up for their peers. And while the bullying didn't disappear overnight, Tyler felt more empowered and less alone, knowing that he had a community of support behind him.

Tyler's story is a powerful example of how one person's voice can make a difference in the fight against cyberbullying. By speaking up, seeking help, and mobilizing others to join the cause, we can create a safer, more compassionate digital world for everyone.

The Responsibility of Sharing: Ethics in the Digital Age

In the age of social media and instant messaging, sharing has never been easier. With only a few clicks, we can broadcast our thoughts, feelings, and experiences to a global audience—and consume an endless stream of content from others in return.

However, with great sharing power comes great responsibility. In a world where misinformation, hate speech, and invasion of privacy are just a share button away, it's more important than ever to approach our digital interactions with an ethical mindset.

So, what does it mean to share responsibly and ethically in the digital age? Here are a few key principles to keep in mind:

- **Verify before you amplify:** Before you hit "share" on that viral news story or shocking meme, take a moment to fact-check it from reputable sources. Don't contribute to the spread of misinformation or false rumors.

- **Consider the impact of your words:** Is what you're sharing likely to hurt, offend, or demean someone else? Could it be triggering or traumatic for certain audiences? Aim to uplift and inform, not tear down or harm.

- **Respect others' privacy:** Just because you have access to someone's personal information or private messages doesn't mean you have the right to share them without consent. Be mindful of others' boundaries and privacy settings.

- **Give credit where it's due:** If you're sharing someone else's work or ideas, make sure to give them proper attribution and credit. Don't pass off others' intellectual property as your own.

- **Use your platform for good:** If you have a large following or influential voice online, consider using it to raise awareness about important issues, amplify marginalized voices, and spread messages of positivity and social change.

 Case Study 23: The Viral Video Gone Wrong

Lina, a 19-year-old college student, was scrolling through her social media feeds one day when she came across a shocking video. It appeared to show a group of teenagers brutally attacking a homeless man in a park, laughing and jeering as they kicked and punched him.

Outraged and heartbroken, Lina immediately hit "share" on the video, adding a caption expressing her disgust and calling for the attackers to be brought to justice. Within hours, the video had gone viral, racking up millions of views and sparking a heated online debate.

However, as the story continued to unfold, new details emerged that complicated the narrative. It turned out that the video had been heavily edited and taken out of context. The "attackers" were actually actors filming a scene for a student film project, and the "victim" was a paid performer.

Lina was horrified to realize that she had contributed to the spread of misinformation and false outrage. She deleted her post and issued an apology, but the damage had already been done. The story had taken on a life of its own, and the student filmmakers were facing a barrage of online harassment and threats.

Lina's experience is a cautionary tale about the power and pitfalls of viral sharing in the digital age. In the heat of the moment, it can be tempting to react and share without fully verifying or understanding the context of what we're seeing. But by taking a beat to fact-check and consider the potential impact of our words, we can help create a more responsible and ethical online culture.

Consent and Content: Navigating Legalities Online

The digital world may feel like a lawless frontier at times, but the reality is that our online actions have real-world legal consequences. From copyright infringement to defamation to revenge porn, there are a host of legal issues that can arise from the content we create and share online.

Consent is one of the most critical legal concepts to understand in the digital age. Just like in the physical world, we need to obtain clear, affirmative consent before engaging in certain online activities—especially those that involve other people's personal information, intellectual property, or intimate content.

So, what does consent look like in the digital realm? Here are a few key principles to keep in mind:

- **Get permission before using others' content:** If you want to use someone else's photos, videos, or written work in your own posts or projects, make sure to get their explicit permission first. Don't assume that just because something is publicly available online, it's fair game to use without consent.

- **Be mindful of others' privacy:** Before posting or sharing content that involves other people, consider whether you have their consent to do so. This is especially important when it comes to sensitive or private information, such as someone's home address, medical history, or intimate photos.

- **Understand the legal implications of your words:** Freedom of speech is a fundamental right, but it's not absolute. Be aware that certain types of online speech—such as defamation, hate speech, or threats—can have legal consequences.

- **Know your rights as a content creator:** If you create original content online, it's important to understand your intellectual property rights and how to protect them. Consider using licenses or watermarks to clarify how others can (and can't) use your work.

- **When in doubt, seek legal guidance:** If you're unsure about the legal implications of a particular online action or piece of content, don't hesitate to seek advice from a qualified legal professional.

Case Study 24: The Copyright Conundrum

Ayman, a 20-year-old graphic design student, had always dreamed of starting his own online store selling his original artwork and designs. He spent months creating a beautiful collection of digital prints, phone cases, and T-shirts featuring his unique illustrations and patterns.

When he finally launched his store, Ayman was thrilled to see his products gaining traction online. But his excitement quickly turned to horror when he discovered that another online retailer had started selling products featuring his exact design—without his permission or knowledge.

Ayman reached out to the retailer and demanded that they remove his stolen designs from their site, but they claimed that since he had posted his artwork on social media, it was fair game for anyone to use and profit from. Ayman was devastated and felt like his hard work and creativity had been violated.

After doing some research and seeking legal advice, Ayman learned that he did, in fact, have intellectual property rights over his original designs. He sent the retailer a formal cease-and-desist letter and filed a copyright infringement complaint with their web hosting service. Eventually, the retailer agreed to remove Ayman's designs and compensate him for the unauthorized use.

Ayman's experience is a powerful reminder of the importance of understanding and protecting our legal rights in the digital age. By being proactive about seeking consent, respecting others' intellectual property, and standing up for our own creative work, we can help create a more ethical and equitable online ecosystem.

Digital Activism: Using Your Voice for Good

In a world where injustice, inequality, and misinformation run rampant, it can be easy to feel powerless or paralyzed in the face of daunting global challenges. But as digital citizens, we have more power than we realize to make a positive impact on the world around us.

Enter the world of digital activism—the use of digital tools and platforms to advocate for social, political, and environmental change. From hashtag campaigns and online petitions to virtual protests and crowdfunding drives, there are countless ways to use our online voices to fight for the causes we believe in.

So, how can we be effective digital activists? Here are a few key strategies:

- **Educate yourself:** Before you start advocating for a particular issue or cause, make sure you have a deep understanding of the context, history, and nuances involved. Seek out diverse perspectives and reputable sources of information to inform your views.

- **Choose your battles:** There are countless worthy causes to fight for, but it's important to focus your energy and attention on the issues that matter most to you. Consider your personal values, experiences, and areas of expertise when deciding where to direct your activism.

- **Amplify marginalized voices:** One of the most powerful things we can do as digital activists is to use our platforms to elevate the voices and experiences of those who have been historically silenced or marginalized. Seek out and share content from diverse creators and communities.

- **Be strategic in your messaging:** When crafting your activist content, consider your audience, your goals, and the most effective ways to communicate your message. Use clear, compelling language and visuals to capture attention and inspire action.

- **Take your activism offline:** While digital activism can be incredibly powerful, it's important to remember that real change happens in the physical world, too. Look for ways to translate your online advocacy into offline action, whether it's attending protests, volunteering for local organizations, or having difficult conversations with friends and family.

 Case Study 25: The Hashtag Hero

Imani, a 20-year-old college student, had always been passionate about social justice and equality. Growing up as a Black woman in America, she had experienced firsthand the impact of systemic racism and discrimination, and she was determined to use her voice to make a difference.

When the Black Lives Matter protests erupted across the country in the summer of 2020, Imani knew she had to take action. She started by attending local protests and marches but quickly realized that she could have an even broader impact by leveraging her social media platform.

Imani started using hashtags like #BlackLivesMatter to amplify the voices and demands of the movement. She shared powerful images and stories from the front lines of the protests and used her platform to educate her followers about the history and impact of police brutality and systemic racism.

As her activism gained traction online, Imani started to receive pushback and harassment from those who disagreed with her views. But she refused to be silenced. She continued to speak out, even as the threats and trolling intensified, and inspired countless others to join the fight for racial justice.

Imani's story is a powerful example of how one person's digital activism can have a ripple effect that reaches far beyond their immediate network. By using her voice and platform to raise awareness, challenge oppressive systems, and mobilize others to take action, she helped create a more just and equitable world—one hashtag at a time.

The Golden Rule Goes Digital: Treating Others with Respect Online

We all learned the Golden Rule as kids: "Treat others as you want to be treated." But in the Wild West of the digital world, it can be easy to forget this simple but profound principle of human decency.

Behind every screen and avatar is a real person with real feelings, hopes, and struggles. When we interact with others online, it's crucial that we approach those interactions with the same level of respect, empathy, and kindness that we would expect in face-to-face communication.

So, what does it look like to apply the Golden Rule to our digital lives? Here are a few key principles to keep in mind:

- **Assume good intent:** It's easy to misinterpret tone or intent in online communication, so always give others the benefit of the doubt. Assume that they are coming from a place of goodwill, even if their words or actions are imperfect.

- **Communicate with clarity and kindness:** Aim for clear, concise, and respectful language when expressing yourself online. Avoid sarcasm, snark, or passive-aggression, which can easily be misconstrued or cause hurt feelings.

- **Listen before you react:** If someone says or does something online that upsets you, take a moment to breathe and reflect before responding. Try to understand where they are coming from and approach the situation with curiosity and empathy rather than defensiveness or aggression.

- **Apologize and make amends:** If you mess up and say or do something hurtful online, don't be afraid to own up to it and apologize sincerely. Look for ways to make amends and rebuild trust, just as you would in a face-to-face relationship.

- **Spread positivity and gratitude:** Use your online presence to spread joy, appreciation, and encouragement to others. Share uplifting stories, express gratitude for the people and experiences that enrich your life, and look for opportunities to make someone else's day a little brighter

 Case Study 26: The Online Olive Branch

Theo and Stella had been best friends since childhood, but a heated argument on social media had left their relationship in tatters. It all started when Theo posted a controversial political meme that Stella found offensive and hurtful. She called him out in the comments, and the conversation quickly devolved into a flurry of angry jabs and personal attacks.

For weeks after the incident, Theo and Stella avoided each other online and in real life. They both felt hurt, misunderstood, and resentful, but neither knew how to bridge the gap and repair their friendship.

Finally, Theo decided to extend an olive branch. He sent Stella a private message apologizing for his role in the argument and asking if they could talk things out. At first, Stella was hesitant and defensive, but as they started to communicate with more openness and empathy, she began to soften.

Over the course of several honest, vulnerable conversations, Theo and Stella were able to see each other's perspectives more clearly. They realized that their argument had been fueled by misunderstandings and knee-jerk reactions rather than a fundamental difference in values. They apologized for the hurtful things they had said and committed to treating each other with more respect and care moving forward.

Theo and Stella's story is a reminder that even in the digital age, the Golden Rule still applies. By approaching our online interactions with the same level of compassion, humility, and forgiveness that we would want for ourselves, we can build stronger, more resilient relationships—both on and off the screen.

At the end of the day, the ethics of our online behavior come down to a simple but profound choice: What kind of digital world do we want to create? One fueled by toxicity, division, and mistrust? Or one anchored in empathy, responsibility, and shared humanity?

As digital citizens, we have the power to shape the online landscape with every post, comment, and interaction. By approaching our digital lives with intention, integrity, and a commitment to the greater good, we can harness the incredible potential of technology to connect, inspire, and transform our world for the better.

So, let us move forward with courage and compassion, using our digital powers for good and leaving a legacy of positive change in our wake. Together, we can create a more ethical, equitable, and empowering online culture—one click at a time.

Chapter 7

Critical Thinking Skills for the Digital World

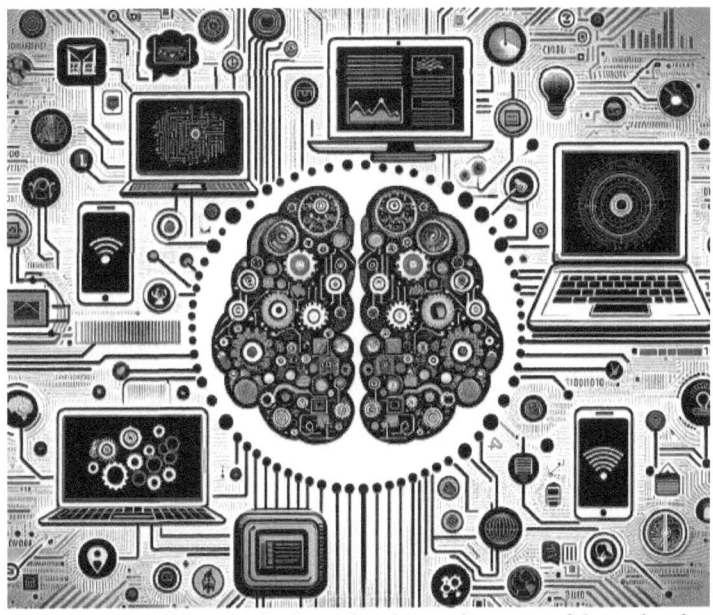

"Question fiercely, think independently. In the ocean of digital information, be the navigator who seeks truth." – LLR Academy

In a world where information is just a click away, developing sharp critical thinking skills is more important than ever. The digital landscape is a vast and complex ecosystem, teeming with a dizzying array of sources, perspectives, and agendas. As a modern teen, navigating this terrain can feel like trying to find a needle in a haystack—or worse, like being lost in a hall of mirrors where everything is distorted, and nothing is quite what it seems.

But fear not, intrepid explorer! With the right tools and techniques, you can learn to cut through the noise, spot the spin, and uncover the truth (or at least get a lot closer to it). In this chapter, we'll dive deep into the art and science of critical thinking in the digital age. From evaluating sources and dissecting arguments to conducting deep research and understanding bias, we'll equip you with a powerful tool kit for making sense of the online world. Grab your magnifying glass and your thinking cap, and let's get started!

Questioning the Source: Critical Evaluation of Online Information

Picture this: You're scrolling through your social media feed when you come across a shocking headline. "New study proves that eating chocolate can cure cancer!" the post proclaims, with a link to an article on a website you've never heard of. What do you do? If your first instinct is to hit that share button and spread the news far and wide, you might want to pump the brakes. In the digital age, not all information is created equal—and it's up to us to separate the wheat from the chaff.

 Case Study 27: The Chocolate Cure Conundrum

Lilly, a curious 15-year-old, came across a viral post claiming that eating chocolate could cure cancer. Excited by the prospect, she was about to share the article with her friends and family. But then she remembered the critical thinking skills she had been learning in school. She decided to investigate further before spreading the news.

Lilly first looked at the website where the article was posted. She noticed that it was a blog with no clear author or credentials. The site was filled with ads and sensational headlines, which raised red flags. She then googled the claim and found that no reputable medical organizations or journals had published anything about chocolate curing cancer.

By taking a few minutes to question the source and do some additional research, Lilly avoided falling for and spreading misinformation. She realized that if something sounds too good to be true, it probably is.

The first step in critically evaluating online information is to question the source. Who is behind this website or social media account? What are their credentials and expertise? What is their agenda or bias? A quick Google search or peek at the "About" page can often reveal a lot about the credibility and trustworthiness of a source.

Next, take a closer look at the information itself. Is it supported by credible evidence, such as peer-reviewed studies or expert analysis? Or, is it based on anecdotes, opinions, or cherry-picked data? Be wary of sources that make bold claims without backing them up or rely on emotional appeals rather than facts and logic.

Finally, consider the context and framing of the information. Is it presented in a balanced and objective way, or is it skewed to push a particular viewpoint? Are there other perspectives or counterarguments that are being ignored or dismissed? By asking these kinds of critical questions, you can start to develop a more nuanced and accurate understanding of the information you encounter online.

Logic and Lies: Dissecting Arguments on Social Media

Social media is a battleground of ideas, where arguments and debates rage on everything from politics to pop culture. But amidst all the noise and fury, it can be hard to tell the difference between a sound argument and a sneaky fallacy. That's where the art of logical reasoning comes in.

 Case Study 28: The Great Vaccine Debate

Aaron, a 16-year-old, was scrolling through his social media feed when he came across a heated debate about vaccines. One user argued that vaccines were dangerous and caused autism, while another countered that vaccines were safe and necessary for public health.

Aaron noticed that the anti-vaccine argument relied heavily on anecdotal evidence and emotional appeals rather than scientific data. The user kept saying things like, "I know someone whose child got autism right after being vaccinated," and "Big Pharma is just trying to make money off of us!"

On the other hand, the pro-vaccine argument cited numerous peer-reviewed studies and expert opinions from medical organizations. The user also pointed out the logical fallacies in the anti-vaccine argument, such as the false causation between vaccines and autism.

By analyzing the structure and reasoning of each argument, Aaron saw that the pro-vaccine position was much stronger, and more evidence based. He realized that just because someone says something passionately doesn't mean it's true.

At its core, logical reasoning is about evaluating the structure and validity of arguments. A strong argument is one that follows a clear chain of logic, with premises that support its conclusion. A weak or fallacious argument, on the other hand, relies on faulty reasoning, false assumptions, or manipulative tactics to make its case.

One common fallacy to watch out for on social media is the ad hominem attack, where someone tries to discredit an argument by attacking the character or motives of the person making it rather than addressing the substance of the argument itself. For example, "Of course he would say that; he's just a shill for the oil industry!" This kind of personal attack may be emotionally satisfying, but it doesn't actually prove or disprove the argument at hand.

By learning to spot these kinds of logical fallacies and rhetorical tricks, you can become a more savvy and critical consumer of social media discourse. But it's not just about poking holes in other people's arguments—it's also about constructing your own arguments in a clear, logical, and persuasive way. By backing up your claims with credible evidence, anticipating counterarguments, and avoiding fallacies and biases, you can make your voice heard in the digital marketplace of ideas.

Beyond the First Page of Results: Deep Dive Research Skills

When it comes to researching a topic online, it's easy to fall into the trap of the "first page fallacy," that is, assuming that the top results on a search engine like Google are the most credible and comprehensive sources on the subject. But as any seasoned researcher knows, the real gems are often buried deeper in the digital stacks.

Case Study 29: The Climate Change Deep Dive

Maren, a 17-year-old environmental activist, wanted to learn more about the scientific consensus on climate change. She started by googling "climate change" and reading through the first few pages of results. She found a lot of general information and news articles but nothing that really dug into the nitty-gritty of the science.

So, Maren decided to go deeper. She searched for "peer-reviewed studies on climate change" and found a wealth of academic papers and meta-analyses. She also discovered specialized science news sites and blogs that provided in-depth coverage of the latest research.

As she read through these sources, Maren started to notice patterns and consistencies in the data and conclusions. She found that the vast majority of climate scientists agreed that human activities were driving global warming and that the evidence for this was overwhelming.

By going beyond the first page of results and seeking out specialized, in-depth sources, Maren was able to develop a much more robust and nuanced understanding of the science of climate change. She felt more confident in her ability to discuss the issue with others and advocate for policy changes.

To conduct truly deep and rigorous research, you need to go beyond the first page of results and explore a wide range of sources and perspectives. This might mean digging into academic databases, scouring specialized forums and discussion boards, or even reaching out to experts and authorities in the field.

One powerful tool for deep-dive research is the use of advanced search operators. You can narrow your search results to the most relevant and credible sources by using specific keywords and phrases. For example, adding "site:edu" to your search query will limit the results to educational institutions, while using quotation marks around a phrase will search for that exact wording.

Another key strategy is to cross-reference and corroborate information from multiple sources. Don't just rely on one website or article, no matter how authoritative it may seem. Look for patterns and consistencies across different sources, and be skeptical of outliers or contradictory claims.

By developing these deep-dive research skills, you'll be able to uncover hidden gems of knowledge and insight that most people miss. And in a world where surface-level information is cheap and abundant, that kind of depth and rigor is a valuable commodity indeed.

The Power of Perspective: Understanding Bias in Digital Content

In the digital age, it's not just the information itself that matters—it's also the lens through which that information is presented. Every piece of content we encounter online, from news articles to social media posts to search results, is shaped by the perspectives, values, and biases of its creators and curators.

 Case Study 30: The Political Echo Chamber

Ethan, an 18-year-old first-time voter, was trying to learn more about the candidates in an upcoming election. He started by following some political pages and groups on social media that aligned with his own views. Soon, his feed was filled with posts and articles that reinforced his existing beliefs and made the opposing candidate look bad.

Ethan noticed that he wasn't seeing any posts that challenged his assumptions or presented the other side's perspective. He realized that he was in a kind of "echo chamber"—a digital space where his own views were amplified, and alternative views were filtered out.

So, Ethan decided to burst his bubble. He sought out reputable news sources from across the political spectrum and read articles that presented both sides of the issues. He also joined some online discussion forums where people with diverse views engaged in respectful, evidence-based debates.

By intentionally exposing himself to a range of perspectives, Ethan was able to develop a more nuanced and balanced understanding of the election. He felt more prepared to cast an informed vote based on the full complexity of the issues, not just his own preconceptions.

Some biases are more obvious than others. A political website that openly promotes a particular party or ideology, for example, clearly comes from a specific point of view. However, other biases can be more subtle and insidious. The algorithms that power our search engines and social media feeds, for instance, are designed to show us content that aligns with our existing beliefs and interests—a phenomenon known as the "filter bubble."

To be a truly critical thinker in the digital world, it's essential to understand and account for these biases in the content we consume. This means looking beyond the surface level of what's being said and asking deeper questions about who is saying it, why they're saying it, and what perspectives or voices might be missing from the conversation.

One powerful tool for uncovering bias is to actively seek out diverse perspectives on a given topic. Don't just rely on your usual go-to sources or echo chambers—make a point of exploring content from different political, cultural, and ideological viewpoints. By exposing yourself to a range of perspectives, you can start to develop a more nuanced and comprehensive understanding of the issues at stake.

Ultimately, understanding bias in digital content is not about achieving some mythical state of perfect objectivity or neutrality. Rather, it's about developing the critical thinking skills to navigate a complex and often contradictory information landscape and to make informed, responsible choices about what to believe and how to act. In a world where perspective is power, that kind of discernment is more important than ever.

Constructive Skepticism: A Teen's Guide to Questioning Authority Online

As digital natives, today's teens are often more tech-savvy and plugged-in than their parents and teachers. But when it comes to navigating the online world, that digital fluency can sometimes translate into a kind of blind trust in the authority of the internet itself. After all, if it's on the first page of Google, it must be true, right?

Wrong. As we've seen throughout this chapter, the digital landscape is full of misinformation, bias, and hidden agendas. To be a truly critical thinker in this environment, it's essential to cultivate a healthy sense of skepticism and a willingness to question authority—even (and especially) when that authority comes in the form of a sleek website or a viral social media post.

Case Study 31: The Influencer Illusion

Olivia, a 14-year-old aspiring artist, loved following her favorite Instagram influencers for inspiration and advice. One influencer in particular, who had over a million followers, always seemed to have the perfect life—traveling to exotic locations, wearing designer clothes, and creating stunning artwork.

Olivia tried to emulate this influencer's style and techniques, but she always felt like she was falling short. She started to feel discouraged and wondered if she had what it took to be a "real" artist.

One day, Olivia came across an exposé article that revealed the truth behind this influencer's perfect image. It turned out that many of her photos were heavily edited and staged and that she had a team of assistants and sponsors helping her behind the scenes. Her "effortless" lifestyle was actually the result of a carefully curated brand.

This realization was a wake-up call for Olivia. She started to question the authenticity of the other influencers and authorities she followed online. She realized that just because someone had a large following or a polished image didn't mean they were always telling the whole truth.

Olivia began to approach her online influences with a more critical eye. She looked for red flags like sponsored content, edited photos, and inconsistencies in their stories. She also started to seek out a more diverse range of voices and perspectives beyond the mainstream influencer bubble.

By cultivating a healthy skepticism of online authority, Olivia was able to develop a more authentic and grounded sense of her own artistic identity. She realized that true creativity and success came from within, not from imitating someone else's carefully curated image.

But what does constructive skepticism look like in practice? It starts with a fundamental shift in mindset—from passive consumer to active inquirer. Instead of simply accepting information at face value, a constructive skeptic asks probing questions and looks for evidence to support or refute claims. They don't just take an expert's word for it but seek out multiple perspectives and sources to get a fuller picture.

This doesn't mean being cynical or dismissive of all authority figures or institutions. Rather, it means approaching them with a spirit of respectful but rigorous inquiry and being willing to hold them accountable when they fall short. It means recognizing that even the most credentialed and respected sources can be fallible or biased and that the truth often lies somewhere in the messy, nuanced middle.

By cultivating these habits of constructive skepticism, teens can become more discerning and empowered digital citizens—not just consumers of information but active participants in shaping the online world for the better.

Creating Your Critical Thinking Toolkit: Resources Every Teen Needs

We've covered a lot of ground in this chapter–from evaluating sources and dissecting arguments to understanding bias and questioning authority. But the journey of critical thinking is never really finished; it's a lifelong process of learning, growth, and discovery.

To support you on that journey, here are some essential resources to add to your critical thinking tool kit:

- **Fact-checking websites:** Sites like Snopes, PolitiFact, and Fact Check.org are great places to go when you're not sure if a claim or story is true. They provide in-depth, nonpartisan analysis of viral rumors, urban legends, and political claims.

- **Media literacy organizations:** Groups like the News Literacy Project, the Center for Media Literacy, and the Digital Citizenship Institute offer a wealth of resources and training on how to be a savvy and responsible consumer of media in the digital age.

- **Critical thinking courses and programs:** Many schools, libraries, and community organizations offer courses and workshops on critical thinking skills. Look for opportunities to deepen your knowledge and practice your skills in a structured, supportive environment.

- **Online discussion forums:** Websites like Reddit, Quora, and Stack Exchange can be great places to engage in substantive, respectful dialogue on a wide range of topics. Look for forums that encourage critical thinking and evidence-based discussion, and be an active participant in shaping the conversation.

- **Diverse media sources:** Make a point of seeking out news and information from a range of reputable sources across different political, cultural, and ideological perspectives. The more diverse your media diet, the more well-rounded and nuanced your understanding will be.

Remember, building your critical thinking skills is not a one-time event but a lifelong process. By continuously seeking out new knowledge, engaging in respectful dialogue, and reflecting on your own biases and assumptions, you can become a more discerning, empowered, and responsible digital citizen. Keep asking questions, keep exploring new ideas, and keep pushing yourself to think deeper and more critically about the world around you. The future of our digital democracy depends on it.

Chapter 8

Preparing for Digital Adulthood

"Step into your digital future with wisdom and courage. Equip yourself today for the world you'll navigate tomorrow." -- LLR Academy

As you navigate the complex digital landscape of your teenage years, it's easy to get caught up in the here and now. But while the digital world can often feel like a realm of instant gratification and fleeting distractions, it's important to remember that the choices you make and the habits you cultivate online today can have a profound impact on your future.

In this chapter, we'll explore what it means to prepare for digital adulthood—to think strategically and proactively about your online presence, digital skills, and relationship with technology as you look ahead to college, career, and beyond. From crafting a compelling digital brand to mastering the art of online content creation, from developing the skills you'll need to thrive in a rapidly evolving digital economy to knowing when to unplug and prioritize your personal growth, we'll cover all the essential elements of building a successful and fulfilling digital future

Digital Branding: Crafting Your Online Presence for the Future

In the digital age, your online presence is more than just a collection of posts and profiles—it's an extension of your identity, a representation of your values, skills, and aspirations. Just as you might carefully curate your resume or put thought into what you wear to a job interview, it's important to be intentional and strategic about how you present yourself online.

This is where the concept of digital branding comes in—the process of crafting a cohesive, authentic, and compelling online presence that showcases who you are, what you stand for, and what you have to offer. Whether you're looking to impress college admissions officers, catch the eye of potential employers, or simply build a positive reputation in your personal and professional networks, a strong digital brand can open doors and create opportunities.

Case Study 32: The LinkedIn Launchpad

London, a high school senior, was starting to think about her plans for after graduation. She knew she wanted to go to college and eventually start a career in marketing, but she wasn't sure how to stand out in a sea of applicants and job seekers.

That's when London learned about the power of LinkedIn. She realized that by creating a compelling LinkedIn profile and actively engaging with the marketing community on the site, she could start building her digital brand and making connections that could help her achieve her goals.

By the time London graduated from high school, she had already laid the foundation for a strong digital brand in her chosen field. She had a network of mentors and contacts, a portfolio of relevant experiences and skills, and a clear sense of direction for her future. All thanks to the power of intentional, strategic digital branding.

From Digital Consumer to Creator: Making Your Mark Online

In the early days of the internet, most of us were content to be passive consumers of digital content. However, as the digital landscape has evolved, so have the opportunities for individuals to become active creators and contributors in their own right.

From starting a blog or podcast to launching a YouTube channel or developing an app, there are countless ways for teens to make their mark online and share their unique voices with the world—and the benefits of doing so go far beyond just creative expression. By developing digital creation skills and building a portfolio of work, you can set yourself up for success in a wide range of careers and industries.

Case Study 33: The Podcast Prodigy

Dax, a 16-year-old with a passion for storytelling, had always dreamed of having his own radio show. But with no connections in the industry and limited resources, he wasn't sure how to make that dream a reality.

That's when Dax discovered the world of podcasting. With just a microphone, a computer, and some free recording software, he realized he could create and distribute his own audio content to a global audience.

Dax started by researching popular podcasts in his niche and studying their formats, styles, and production techniques. He invested in a quality microphone and taught himself how to use audio editing software. Then, he launched his own podcast, featuring interviews with local entrepreneurs and thought leaders.

At first, Dax's listenership was small. However, as he continued to produce high-quality content and promote his show on social media, his audience began to grow. By the time he graduated high school, Dax's podcast had thousands of regular listeners and had even attracted sponsorships from local businesses.

Dax's story showcases the incredible power of digital creation to turn passions into professions. By taking the initiative to develop his skills and share his unique voice online, Liam was able to build a platform and a reputation that would serve him well in his future career pursuits.

The Future of Work: Skills You Need in a Digital Economy

As the world becomes increasingly digitized and automated, the nature of work is changing rapidly. To thrive in this digital economy, it's essential for teens to start developing the skills and mindsets that will be in high demand in the years to come.

Key skills for the future of work include digital literacy, adaptability and continuous learning, collaboration and communication, creative problem-solving, and entrepreneurship and self-management. By focusing on these key skill areas and staying attuned to the changing landscape of work, you can position yourself for success in the digital economy of the future.

 ### Case Study 34: The Digital Skill Set

Emma, a 17-year-old aspiring software engineer, knew that to be competitive in the tech industry, she would need more than just a degree. She would need a diverse set of digital skills and the ability to adapt and learn continuously.

So, Emma set out to build her digital skill set from the ground up. She took online courses in programming languages like Python and JavaScript and practiced her coding skills through hackathons and personal projects. She also developed her skills in data analysis, user experience design, and project management through internships and volunteer work.

But Emma didn't just focus on technical skills. She also sought out opportunities to develop her soft skills, like communication, collaboration, and creative problem-solving. She joined a robotics club at school, where she worked in teams to design and build complex machines. She also started a blog where she shared her experiences and insights on technology and innovation.

By the time Emma entered college, she had a robust set of digital skills and a strong portfolio of projects and experiences. She was well-equipped to thrive in a rapidly changing digital economy and had a competitive edge in the job market.

Emma's story illustrates the importance of proactively developing a diverse set of digital skills, both technical and soft, to adapt and succeed in the future of work. By taking control of her own skill development and staying curious and open to new learning opportunities, Emma positioned herself for a bright and fulfilling career in the digital age

Protecting Your Data: Security Skills for the Modern Teen

In this context, developing strong digital security skills is no longer a nice-to-have—it's a critical life skill for anyone who wants to protect their privacy, safety, and well-being in the digital age. As a teen, it's especially important to be proactive about safeguarding your data and taking control of your online presence.

Key tips include using strong and unique passwords, enabling two-factor authentication, being cautious about what you share online, keeping your software and devices up-to-date, and using secure networks and connections. By developing these digital security habits and staying vigilant about protecting your data, you can help safeguard your online presence and minimize the risk of digital threats.

Case Study 35: The Hacker Hunter

Austin, a 15-year-old tech enthusiast, had always been fascinated by the world of cybersecurity. He loved learning about the latest hacking techniques and the ways that individuals and organizations could protect themselves from digital threats.

So, when Austen's school announced a cybersecurity competition, he jumped at the chance to put his skills to the test. The competition involved a series of challenges, from identifying and fixing vulnerabilities in a mock website to decrypting coded messages.

Austen spent weeks preparing for the competition. He studied cybersecurity best practices, learned new programming languages, and even built his own tools for detecting and mitigating digital threats. On the day of the competition, he was ready to take on any challenge.

To his surprise, Austen won first place in the competition. His skills and preparation had paid off, and he had proven himself to be a rising star in the world of cybersecurity.

But Austen's journey didn't stop there. Inspired by his success, he started a cybersecurity club at his school, where he taught his peers about digital security and helped them develop their own skills. He also began volunteering with local organizations, offering his expertise to help protect their digital assets and data.

Austen's story showcases the incredible potential of developing digital security skills at a young age. By taking an interest in cybersecurity and proactively building his knowledge and abilities, Austen not only protected himself and his own data but also made a positive impact on his community and set himself up for a successful career in a rapidly growing field.

Lifelong Digital Learning: Keeping Up with the Pace of Technology

In a world where technology is advancing at breakneck speed, the ability to keep learning and adapting is no longer optional. It's a critical survival skill that will determine your success and fulfillment in both your personal and professional life. The good news is that with the right mindset and strategies, lifelong digital learning can be a fun and rewarding journey rather than a daunting chore.

Key tips include embracing a growth mindset, staying curious and open-minded, taking advantage of online learning resources, engaging in hands-on learning and experimentation, and seeking out mentors and learning communities. By embracing lifelong digital learning as a mindset and a habit, you can position yourself for success and fulfillment in a rapidly changing world

 ### Case Study 36: The Lifelong Learner

Sophia, a 20-year-old college student, had always been a curious and driven learner. But as she entered the workforce, she quickly realized that the skills she had learned in school were only the beginning. To keep up with the rapid pace of technological change and stay competitive in her field, she would need to commit to lifelong learning.

Sophia started by setting learning goals for herself each month. She identified areas where she wanted to grow her skills, like data visualization or digital marketing, and sought out online courses and resources to help her learn. She also attended industry conferences and workshops to stay up to date on the latest trends and best practices.

But Sophia didn't just rely on formal learning opportunities. She also embraced a mindset of continuous experimentation and hands-on learning. She started a side project where she could apply her new skills in a real-world context and sought out feedback and mentorship from more experienced professionals in her field.

Over time, Sophia's commitment to lifelong learning paid off. She became known as a go-to expert in her company for the latest digital tools and strategies and was able to take on increasingly complex and impactful projects. As the technology landscape continued to evolve, Sophia was well-equipped to adapt and thrive.

Sophia's story illustrates the power of embracing lifelong digital learning as a mindset and a habit. By setting learning goals, seeking out diverse learning opportunities, and applying her skills through hands-on projects, Sophia positioned herself for long-term success and fulfillment in a rapidly changing world. Her curiosity, adaptability, and proactive approach to skill-building became her greatest assets in navigating the digital age.

The Art of Digital Detachment: Knowing When to Log Off for Personal Growth

As important as digital skills and lifelong learning are, they're only one part of the equation when it comes to personal growth and fulfillment. Equally important is the ability to detach from technology when needed to create space for reflection, rest, and renewal.

Key tips include setting boundaries and limits, prioritizing face-to-face interactions, practicing mindfulness and presence, pursuing offline hobbies and interests, embracing solitude and reflection, and leading by example. By creating space for offline experiences, face-to-face interactions, and inner reflection, you can cultivate a more holistic and grounded sense of self in the digital age.

Case Study 37: The Digital Detoxer

Evan, an 18-year-old high school senior, was always glued to his screens. Whether he was scrolling through social media, playing video games, or binge-watching the latest streaming series, Evan spent most of his free time online. But as his screen time began to take a toll on his sleep, relationships, and overall well-being, Evan knew something needed to change.

So, Evan decided to embark on a digital detox. For one month, he committed to significantly reducing his screen time and focusing on offline activities and experiences. He started by setting clear boundaries around his technology use, like no screens before bedtime and device-free meals with family and friends.

At first, the digital detox was challenging. Evan felt anxious and disconnected without the constant stimulation of his screens. But as he began to fill his time with other activities, like reading, exercising, and exploring nature, he started to feel a shift. He slept better, felt more present and engaged in his relationships, and discovered new hobbies and passions.

By the end of the month, Evan had gained a new perspective on his relationship with technology. He realized that while the digital world had its benefits, it was equally important to create space for offline experiences and self-reflection. He decided to continue incorporating digital detox practices into his routine, like taking regular screen-free days and setting intentions for his technology use.

Evan's story is a powerful example of the transformative potential of digital detachment. By creating intentional boundaries around his screen time and prioritizing offline experiences, Evan was able to reclaim a sense of balance and well-being in his life. He discovered that true growth and fulfillment come not just from what we do online but from the rich inner world that we cultivate through reflection, connection, and presence.

Evan's digital detox journey became a powerful catalyst for his personal growth and self-discovery. By learning to be intentional and mindful in his relationship with technology, he developed a more grounded and authentic sense of self—one that would serve him well in all areas of his life, both online and off.

Preparing for digital adulthood is a multifaceted and ongoing journey. By crafting a strong digital brand, developing diverse digital skills, embracing lifelong learning, and practicing intentional technology use, you can set yourself up for success and fulfillment in the ever-evolving landscape of the digital age. Remember, your digital life is just one dimension of your overall identity and well-being, so approach it with intention, purpose, and balance. With the right mindset and strategies, you have the power to shape your digital future and thrive in a world of endless possibilities.

CONCLUSION

Final Reflections on Our Journey

In this book, we've explored the many facets of navigating the digital landscape as a modern teen. From developing critical thinking skills and emotional intelligence to managing your online presence and preparing for the future of work, we've covered a wide range of topics and strategies for thriving in the digital age.

But beyond the practical tips and case studies, my hope is that this book has inspired you to approach your digital life with a sense of empowerment, intentionality, and purpose. The digital world is not just a passive backdrop to your life; it's an active and dynamic space where you have the power to learn, create, connect, and make a difference.

As you continue on your digital journey, remember that you are not just a consumer of technology but a creator and innovator in your own right. Your unique voice, perspective, and talents have the potential to shape the digital landscape in meaningful and impactful ways. Whether you're starting a blog, developing an app, or simply sharing your ideas and experiences online, you have the opportunity to leave a positive mark on the world and inspire others to do the same.

At the same time, remember that your digital life is just one dimension of your overall identity and well-being. As important as it is to develop your digital skills and online presence, it's equally important to cultivate your offline relationships, experiences, and sense of self. Make time for face-to-face connections, pursue hobbies and interests that bring you joy, and prioritize self-care and personal growth.

As you navigate the challenges and opportunities of the digital age, keep coming back to your core values, passions, and purpose. Use technology as a tool to enhance and amplify your learning, creativity, and positive impact, but don't let it define or consume you. Set healthy boundaries around your screen time, and be mindful of how your digital habits are affecting your mental, emotional, and physical well-being.

Embrace the art of digital detachment when you need to recharge and reconnect with yourself and others. Take regular breaks from your devices, unplug from social media when it becomes overwhelming, and carve out screen-free time for rest, reflection, and renewal. Seek out mentors, communities, and resources that support your growth and well-being.

Most importantly, trust in your own wisdom, resilience, and potential to thrive in a rapidly changing world. You have the power to shape your own digital destiny and to use technology in ways that align with your values and goals. Don't be afraid to experiment, take risks, and learn from your mistakes—that's how innovation and growth happen.

The digital age may be complex and ever evolving, but with the right mindset, skills, and strategies, you have everything you need to navigate it with confidence, integrity, and purpose. You are part of a generation that has the potential to harness the power of technology for incredibly good—to solve problems, bridge divides, and create a more just and sustainable world.

So, go create the digital life of your dreams—one that is fulfilling, meaningful, and true to who you are. Embrace your role as a digital leader and changemaker, and never underestimate the impact that your unique voice and vision can have. The world is waiting for your light to shine—so let it beam brightly, both online and off.

BONUS EXCERCISES
Engage, Think, Solve

Here are a few more exercises designed for you, aimed at cultivating clarity and critical thinking in the digital age.

These exercises are

- tailored to help you navigate the complexities of modern information environments.

- encourage teenagers to think critically about the information they consume daily, fostering a more discerning approach to navigating digital spaces.

- aim to help teenagers become more discerning readers and thinkers in the digital space, equipping them with the critical skills needed to engage thoughtfully and responsibly with the content they encounter online.

- not only encourage critical analysis and skepticism in evaluating digital content but also help teenagers build the necessary skills to navigate complex media landscapes responsibly.

Exercise 16: The Influencer's Influence

Objective: To analyze how influencers can shape perceptions and decisions through digital media, fostering an awareness of persuasion techniques.

Instructions:

1. Choose a digital influencer that you either follow or know about, and watch or read three of their most recent posts or videos.

2. Analyze the content for the following:

    - What messages are being communicated, both overtly and subtly?

    - Identify any persuasive techniques being used (e.g., appeal to emotion, bandwagon, celebrity endorsement).

    - Consider the potential impact of these messages on their audience.

3. Write a brief critique discussing the effectiveness of the influencer's communication strategies and their potential impact on young people's choices and opinions.

Discussion Points:

- How do influencers affect their audience's views and behaviors?

- Can you identify any biases in how they present information?

- Discuss the responsibility of influencers in shaping public opinion.

Exercise 17: Fact or Opinion?

Objective: This exercise helps distinguish between factual information and opinion, which is crucial in understanding news articles, social media posts, and other digital content.

Instructions:

1. Find three articles or posts on a popular social media platform about a current event.

2. For each article or post, list down three statements.

3. Categorize each statement as a 'fact' or an 'opinion.'

4. Explain why you categorized each statement the way you did.

Discussion Points:

- How easy or difficult was it to distinguish between fact and opinion?

- How might opinions influence your perception of the facts?

Exercise 18: Source Reliability Check

Objective: To develop the ability to evaluate the reliability of different sources, particularly in an online environment where information can vary widely

Instructions:

1. Choose a trending topic and find two different online sources reporting on it—one known for reliability and another that is less well-known or has a reputation for bias.

2. Read both articles and make notes on the following:

    - The main claims each source makes.

    - Any evidence provided to support the claims.

    - The tone of the writing (neutral, biased, sensationalist).

3. Assess which source seems more reliable and justify your decision based on your notes.

Discussion Points:

- What indicators helped you determine the reliability of each source?

- How could biased or unreliable sources impact your understanding of the topic?

Exercise 19: Echo Chamber Escape

Objective: This exercise aims to help teenagers recognize and understand the concept of echo chambers in digital environments, promoting exposure to diverse viewpoints.

Instructions:

1. Identify a topic you feel strongly about and search for articles or social media posts related to this topic.

2. Deliberately find sources or posts that present a view different from your own. Aim for at least two distinct perspectives.

3. Read through these perspectives carefully, and then summarize each viewpoint, noting any new or surprising information.

4. Reflect on your feelings and thoughts about encountering differing opinions. Consider whether and how this activity might affect your views.

Discussion Points:

- How difficult was it to find and engage with opposing viewpoints?

- What did you learn about the topic that you didn't know before?

- How might encountering diverse perspectives be beneficial in understanding complex issues?

Exercise 20: Detecting Misinformation

Objective: To develop skills in identifying and understanding misinformation online, which is vital for navigating today's media landscape.

Instructions:

1. Find an article or social media post that claims to report on a recent event or scientific discovery. Ensure this piece comes from a source that isn't widely recognized for its credibility.

2. Investigate the claim by checking other reputable sources. Look for verification or refutation of the information.

3. Identify any discrepancies between the original article and the information found in more reputable sources.

4. Reflect on the potential dangers of spreading misinformation based on your findings.

Discussion Points:

- What strategies did you use to verify the information?

- How could misinformation about this topic affect public opinion or behavior?

- Discuss the importance of cross-referencing sources before sharing information online.

Exercise 21: Analyzing Digital Debates

Objective: To enhance the ability to critically analyze arguments and rhetoric in online discussions, which often feature complex and polarized opinions.

Instructions:

1. Select a popular online forum or social media platform where people are discussing a controversial issue.

2. Choose two users who represent opposing sides in the debate.

3. Analyze their arguments for logical fallacies, strengths, and weaknesses. Note the use of evidence and emotional appeals.

4. Summarize each side's main points and critique their argumentative methods.

Discussion Points:

- Which argument was more convincing, and why?
- Were there any logical fallacies that weakened the arguments?
- How do the rhetorical strategies used affect the reader's or viewer's perception of the issue?

Exercise 22: Bias Exploration

Objective: To help teenagers identify and understand bias in various media sources, fostering an awareness of how bias can influence information.

Instructions:

1. Choose a current event that is being covered by multiple news outlets.

2. Select articles about this event from three different sources: one known for a conservative bias, one known for a liberal bias, and one that strives for neutrality.

3. Read each article and note the following:

    - How the headline portrays the event

    - Any emotionally charged words used

    - Information that is emphasized or omitted in each article

4. Compare and contrast the three articles, identifying any apparent biases.

Discussion Points:

- How does the bias affect the presentation of the facts?

- Why is it important to recognize media bias when forming opinions?

- How can identifying bias improve your media literacy?

Exercise 23: Real vs. Fake News Quiz

Objective: This exercise aims to sharpen the ability to distinguish between real and fake news stories, an essential skill in today's digital environment.

Instructions:

1. Create a quiz that includes a mixture of real and fake news headlines and brief summaries. Use actual examples from reputable news sites and parody or misinformation sites.

2. Have the teenagers take the quiz, deciding whether each story is real or fake based on the headline and summary alone.

3. Review the answers together, discussing the clues that indicate whether a story is trustworthy or not.

4. Explore strategies for verifying news and the importance of doing so before sharing content online.

Discussion Points:

- What features helped you identify the fake news stories?

- Discuss the impact of fake news on individuals and society.

- What steps can you take to verify the credibility of news before believing or sharing it?

The Author's Message

LLR Academy is an innovative startup where curiosity unlocks opportunity. We are committed to equipping young individuals with the critical skills required to excel in our rapidly changing world. Our team is focused on identifying the specific challenges you face in the digital age and crafting effective strategies to ensure your success.

At LLR Academy, we provide hands-on guidance, interactive activities, and real-world scenarios that foster the development of crucial skills like critical thinking, problem-solving, and effective communication. Our goal is to help young individuals with the necessary tools to confidently and purposefully tackle the complexities of the digital age, empowering them to become assured and autonomous thinkers.

We deeply appreciate our team at LLR Academy who have poured their wisdom and creativity into this book, enriching the young reader's journey and leaving a lasting impact. Our efforts have not only shaped a compelling narrative but have also ignited a vibrant dialogue among curious minds across the globe.

--

Aamir Iqbal | Author and Co-Founder, LLR Academy

To learn more about LLR Academy, visit: www.LearnLeadRise.com

Reader's Review

We Value Your Feedback

Thank you for choosing to explore "The Modern Teen's Handbook: Cultivating Clarity and Critical Thinking in the Digital Age." We hope it has offered you valuable insights and tools to navigate the digital age with confidence. Your feedback is crucial to us and to others who are considering this book. Could you take a few moments to share your thoughts and review?

Click the **link** below or scan the **QR** code to tell us about your experience. Your perspective is incredibly important!

https://www.amazon.com/review/review-your-purchases/?asin=1068857307

Amazon.com

https://www.amazon.ca/review/review-your-purchases/?asin=1068857307

Amazon.ca

Thank you for being an essential part of the LLR Academy community.

Warm regards | The LLR Academy Team

REFRECNCES

Sources and Inspirations

- Goldfield, G. (2023, February 23). *Reducing social media use significantly improves body image in teens, young adults.* American Psychological Association. https://www.apa.org/news/press/releases/2023/02/social-media-body-image

- Gorlick, A. (2016, April 16). *Media multitaskers pay mental price, Stanford study shows.* Stanford News; Stanford University. https://news.stanford.edu/2009/08/24/multitask-research-study-082409/

- Miller, E. (n.d.). *Multitasking: Why your brain can't do it and what you should do about it.* https://radius.mit.edu/sites/default/files/images/Miller%20Multitasking%202017.pdf

- The Value Dividend Strategy – Marius Schober. https://schober.blog/the-value-dividend-strategy/

- Best Websites for Academic Research and Writing. https://phccwritingcenter.org/best-website-for-writing.php

- Breathe Mindfully (52 Essential Life Skills series) - by Mind Brain Emotion. https://mindbrainemotion.com/pages/lifeskills-breathe

BONUS QUOTES

Here are a few more quotes to encourage you all to think more deeply about your interactions with technology and information, fostering a more mindful and empowered approach to their digital lives.

"Empower your mind with curiosity and skepticism—not everything on your screen is as it appears." – LLR Academy

"Embrace technology but guard your attention like treasure. It's the doorway to your mind." – LLR Academy

"Build bridges in the digital world but remember to anchor them in the reality of human connection." – LLR Academy

"Your thoughts shape your world. Equip them with the clarity and critical thinking needed to thrive in the digital age." – LLR Academy

www.ingramcontent.com/pod-product-compliance
Lightning Source LLC
Chambersburg PA
CBHW030439010526
44118CB00011B/706